# SO TOO MY LOVE

ALSO BY HARVEY GOODMAN

*Along the Fortune Trail*

*Winds of Redemption*

# SO TOO MY LOVE

## HARVEY GOODMAN

Jupiter Sky Publishing
Westcliffe

© Copyright 2013, by Harvey Goodman

 Jupiter Sky Publishing LLC
Westcliffe Colorado

All Rights Reserved.

No part of this book may be reproduced, stored in a retrieval system, or transmitted by any means, electronic, mechanical, photocopying, recording, or otherwise, without written permission from the author.

Printed in the United States of America

ISBN: 978-0-578-13333-1

*for Nancy
and Shirley*

*May their descendants live well*

# 1

*Life anew, oh what could be?*
*Volition and chance brought what would be*
*Trust in the Lord for what should be*
*Forever in His hands*

August, 1969. Rain wept into the night sky like tears from heaven, gently enveloping the summer eve with a mercy unknown, unrealized to him. The boy sat in the car, staring vacantly at the red neon Ralph's Market sign which appeared to be melting as the rain cascaded down the windshield before his eyes. While the drops pattered steadily like all the heartbeats of the world, soothing the lonely, he sat catatonic with despair and emptiness, his soul void of all but wrenching gloom and fatalism. His sixteen years of life had brought its share of physical and emotional pain, but nothing of this sort. The worst had always been served up against the beacon of life itself, young and resilient like the shine of a fresh apple, the irrepressible spirit of innocence which could summon magic and wonderment, a context that could always overcome the bad times with the prospect of hope. But the innocence was gone, the curtain pulled back, revealing the realm that accompanies the rush to experience.

The thought finally materialized and dropped on him like the weight of the universe: *What was the point of living if all you did was die in the end?* His resignation was so infinite that it seemed not a thought cast by him, but rather like dung being thrown upon the canvas of his being. That he had no illness or affliction and occupied better circumstances than nearly all of the earth's people was lost to him; his depth of despair was simply relative to his youth and self-absorption.

*Well, what the hell anyway?* He thought absently. The whole summer of '69 had been surreal. On July 20$^{th}$, John Kennedy's dream came to pass as American astronauts were the first to walk on the moon, fulfilling Kennedy's challenge of achieving it before the end of the decade. Then less than three weeks later on August 9$^{th}$, actress Sharon Tate and a few of her high profile friends were all savagely murdered at her house in Benedict Canyon, just six miles from his own home. The fear was palpable in Hollywood and surrounding neighborhoods after the news broke. But the anxiety rolled east like a tidal surge off the Pacific when the very next night a middle aged married couple, Leno and Rosemary LaBianca, were murdered in much the same fashion, stabbed repeatedly in their own home with demonic messages left scrawled on the wall in their blood, and a carving fork left sticking from Leno's mutilated stomach. Most everybody in Los Angeles and beyond had had pause when the two random homes had been breached on successive nights for the sole purpose of gruesomely murdering the occupants. Gun sales soared. No immediate arrests were made. It would be some time yet before authorities would catch up with Charley Manson and his merry flock of whack-job acid zombies.

Then just days after the murders, 'An Aquarian Exposition; 3 Days of Peace and Music', took place in Bethel, New York, like the soothing antithesis to the barbaric acts which had become so newsworthy on the opposite coast. Woodstock became the iconic convulsion of the decade, the crown jewel of the counterculture that spewed the last vestiges of American post WWII values like vomit from a body wracked with the indigestion of the Vietnam War and government corruption. It would turn out that The Domino Theory should have resided only in the pursuit of excellent pizza.

'Make love, not war. Turn on, tune in, and drop out. Love the one you're with'. The drumbeat of the counterculture mantra swept over a generation of youth, ensnaring many with the tentacles of drugs and the notion of a necessary purging of ignorance through new experience, an evolution of nature, like spilled water running its due course. Progressivism! Progressing to where seemed not a relevant question to such relativism. Just get high and go with it, political or not.

Franklin started the car and pulled forward when he saw her exiting the market. Gaby got in and wiped her eyes. "So you'll pick me up at ten tomorrow?" she asked as they began driving the few blocks back to her house on Kling Street. She was nervous. They both were.

"Yeah," he answered. "I've got my football physical in the morning…eight thirty, so I might end up a couple minutes late."

"Please don't be late."

"All right, I'll be on time."

He pulled up in front of her house. They leaned to each other and kissed. "See you tomorrow," she said and started to get out of the car.

"Hey," he called. Gaby looked back as he handed her the three packs of Camels which her father, Francis, had sent them to the store after. "He'll be pissed if you forget these," he said.

"Thanks, baby."

"Hey, where'd you tell them we're going tomorrow?" he suddenly asked.

She looked at him blankly. "I told them we're going to a movie."

"Make sure you pick one they haven't seen."

"There's tons of those. And, that's the least of our worries," she said.

"Yeah," he agreed, feeling slightly moronic. "See you tomorrow… on time."

Gaby closed the door and trotted across the lawn toward her front door, the rain having picked up a bit. Franklin pulled away from the curb and drove slowly down the block.

# 2

Los Angeles (Silverlake) 1957,
The June sun peaked over the neighborhood rooftops, glistening on the morning dew of the front yard grass. The white, clapboard house with a covered wooden porch sat on a street of similar houses. Gaby came out of the bathroom and shuffled into the kitchen, her dark hair hanging onto the shoulders of her pink cotton pajamas. She rubbed the sleep from her eyes and looked around wide-eyed, aware she was the only one awake. She pulled the chair over and crawled up on it then stood eye-level with the freezer door. The closeness to it brought a rise of her senses. She pulled the freezer door open, revealing the carton of vanilla ice cream which seemed to stare back at her, enchanting but forbidding in appearance, an early test of her aversion to risk. In moments more she had a bowl down from the cupboard and dug the ice cream from the carton with the perseverance of a prospector who'd hit the mother lode.

Gaby returned the ice cream to the freezer and was preparing for her indulgence when her brother, Jeff, came into the kitchen. Three years older than Gaby, Jeff was the second youngest of four siblings. Older brothers, Frankie and Billy were still asleep, as were their parents, Francis and Shirley.

Jeff stared at Gaby's ice cream with a contemplative expression. "That's not what you're supposed to have for breakfast," he declared.

"Are you sure?" came her innocent reply, laced with a hint of mischievousness. "We look at the funny papers on Saturday morning. Ice cream goes just right with the funny papers."

Jeff squinted at her logic then opened the freezer and hauled out the ice cream. "Okay, but we have to be quiet. We'll eat it out on the front porch. I'll show you a trick that makes the ice cream better."

"Better?" she asked excitedly. "I want to see that trick."

They sat on the porch swing, Gaby watching intently as Jeff worked at stirring his ice cream with his spoon, the task requiring muscle to maintain the circular motion with the proper spoon depth to ensure efficient processing speed. "You stir it hard like this for a while and it turns creamy," he said. He stopped stirring and chopped the frozen confection a moment before resuming the stir.

Gaby began imitating the ritual, her face a bit contorted with the effort required. "It's hard to stir," she half yelled, her determination growing with the wonder of what it might produce.

"Just keep working at it," Jeff said. "See how mine's getting softer. When that happens it gets easier and easier to stir."

Gaby worked at it, feeling the consistency of the ice cream changing. And it did begin to get easier to stir, *just like Jeff said,* she thought.

A minute later, Jeff looked at hers and gave his Chief Inspector okay. "Yours looks ready," he said, then put his own spoonful to his mouth.

She tried her's and delivered a quick verdict. "Ummm! It's good!" She quickly retrieved another spoonful and began licking it like an ice cream cone. "It's better when it's creamy! That's a good trick!"

They sat and ate their ice cream, staring at the quiet street, oblivious to all but the wonderful treat. Then they saw the older boy pedaling his bike up the middle of the street, his handlebars draped with two canvas bags, puffed out with the load of his route. The stenciling on each bag read, *Los Angeles Times.* The boy pulled a paper and let it fly with a full hurl. The paper landed on the front porch of a neighboring house.

"He's a good shot," Jeff said. They both watched closely as the boy pulled another paper and fired another strike to a house on the other side of the street. "Yeah, I bet I could throw like that...when I'm a little older," Jeff proclaimed. I'm gonna try and get a paper route someday."

Later in the morning, a plan to go to the public pool materialized. Frankie had suggested it to his younger siblings, Billy, Jeff, and Gaby. They readily agreed it was the best idea they'd heard that day. Nothing was more fun than going to the pool and splashing about with all the other kids on a hot, summer day. After a swim, you could lie right on the warm cement poolside and watch all the action, or get a snow cone if you had an extra dime.

"You think we're made of money?" their father, Francis, asked them half-seriously when the request for the price of four admissions surfaced.

"It's twenty-five cents each," Frankie said. "I've got fifty cents, so all we need is fifty cents more...unless you give us the whole dollar...then I could buy us each a candy or snow cone."

As the negotiating continued, the telephone rang. Mother Shirley answered it sweetly as if the president might be calling. "Hello," she said with warmth. Phone calls were fairly infrequent so they generated a bit of excitement when they came. Who might be calling on a Saturday morning suddenly became of interest to the rest of the family as pool negotiations ceased and everybody turned in the direction of where Shirley stood speaking on the phone.

"Yes, hello, Mrs. Turner. I'm fine. How are you?" Shirley said. She listened intently, an expression of intrigue surfacing on her face as the seconds went by. "Why Jeff wears a boy's size six," Shirley said. Jeff suddenly looked around the room like he'd done some dastardly thing along with Colonel Mustard in the Billiard Room. "Really?" Shirley chimed as she reached for the pen and notepad next to the telephone. "Yes, I'm ready." Shirley began writing whatever it was Mrs. Turner was reciting to her. "Yes, we'll be there at noon. Thank you very much Mrs. Turner. Goodbye now."

"What was that?" Francis asked as he lit a Camel.

Shirley was flushed and her words came in a slightly higher pitch than normal. "Her boy Thomas was supposed to be photographed for a catalogue of boy's shoes today, but there was a mix-up and the model shoes are all size six."

"Yeah, so?" Francis said, exhaling a drag.

"Well, Thomas wears a size eight!" Shirley exclaimed, "And Mrs. Turner says Jeff could get the job if he can be there before noon! He just needs to wear nice trousers and dark socks. We'll take extra pairs. It pays twenty dollars!"

Francis's eyes widened. "Twenty bucks? That's my boy! Yesireee, he can be there before noon."

Jeff's face turned to disappointment. "You mean I don't get to go to the pool?" he said like he knew it would never be his twenty bucks.

"You can go to the pool another time…maybe later this afternoon," his father said. "You can't turn down money like that for honest work, Jeff. It sounds like quite an opportunity. You don't look a gift horse in the mouth, son. Who knows? It could lead to bigger jobs. You might end up in the movies or something."

"Oh, it will be fun," Shirley added. "And Gaby is going, too. Mrs. Turner said that an agent for Catalina Swimwear will be there looking for little girl models."

Gaby was the baby of the family by a twist of fate. Shirley had born her three sons by cesarean section and had been advised that she could only have one more without greatly jeopardizing her health. Early in her fourth pregnancy, Shirley fell badly one day and lost the child, a boy. Two years later she became pregnant again and had her last cesarean section. The delivery brought forth the beautiful baby girl with dark hair and blue eyes.

*So Too My Love*

In another part of Los Angeles, on Windsor Street a few blocks from the intersection of Olympic and Crenshaw Boulevards, four-year old Franklin stood watching the water trickling from the hose onto the bare strip of ground between the sidewalk and the street. The ground had turned to a mud hole, which of course was exactly what it was supposed to do. From high above, the late morning sun was already hot, perfect weather for the mud fight which had been going on for some twenty minutes. Franklin was only an interested spectator to the action, though he'd been hit several times by errant mud as the four older boys, including his brother, Brian, slung mud at each other. They laughed and ran around the front yards darting and in and out of the bushes.

Franklin bent down and dug his hand into the mud, enjoying the feel of the goo. He pulled his hand out and picked up the hose, letting the water wash the mud off.

Brother Brian ran up to the mud hole and quickly scooped a handful. "You better not stay here or you're gonna get it!" Brian advised then ran off in chase of a neighbor boy, Jorn Alley, who had been approaching the mud hole to reload. Jorn wasn't fast enough in his escape. Brian's shot hit Jorn in the back of the head and splattered all down his back.

"You dirty rat!' Jorn yelled as he laughed and ran.

Franklin and Brian's mother, Nancy, stuck her head out the front door. "Brian!" she called. "You and Franklin come in now. Go around to the back door and get those muddy clothes off before you step foot in this house…and wash the mud off your feet!"

"Okay," Brian called out.

Their house sat on a corner lot. Brian and Franklin trotted around the side on Ninth Avenue and went to the steps at the back door. Brian looked around for a moment to see if any cars or pedestrians were near. The coast was clear. He pulled off his t-shirt and pushed his shorts down, kicking them to the side. He stood naked. "You better take that shirt off before you go in," he said to Franklin as he grabbed the back door handle. "It's locked!" he cried out in panic.

"Ha ha ha," came the laughing from Jorn Alley and the Ellerhorse brothers as they ran towards Franklin and Brian with their hands full of mud, ready to inflict a final barrage.

Brian leapt from the stoop and sprinted across the yard. The three mud stalkers immediately gave chase, leaving Franklin to watch in awe as his naked seven-year old brother hopped on his bicycle and pedaled like a windmill in a tornado. The mud stalkers chased on foot, all throwing their mud futilely as Brian pulled safely away, his white butt churning and his willie flapping in the breeze.

It no longer mattered to the mud stalkers that they had been unsuccessful in their attempts. They stood and gawked in amazement. "He's riding away naked!" Jorn exclaimed. The boys laughed at the sight of it.

Farther down the street, Brian passed a car coming from the other direction with two women in it. He smiled at them as they stared and began chuckling. Undeterred, Brian turned the corner and pedaled faster up the next street hoping that if he gained enough speed people might not notice he was naked. He rode around the entire block and approached his house with the intent of doing another lap if needed, but the mud stalkers were gone.

# 3

And so it was that Jeff and Gaby began new careers that day as Gaby got the swimsuit job and Jeff's feet were nothing short of brilliant. Mother Shirley quickly came to understand the need for representation and had both Jeff and Gaby signed up with the William Morris Agency in no time. She and Francis took turns taking each to auditions that the agency lined up. Jeff and Gaby both landed more modeling work.

Later that year, Gaby appeared as 'Puddin' in an episode of the first season of 'Leave it to Beaver'. In the episode, Wally and Beaver were tasked with babysitting 'Puddin', who then locked herself in the bathroom and instigated chaos before the fire department came and got her out. She delivered her lines well and proved very convincing in tearing up Wally and the Beav's bathroom.

About that same time, Jeff auditioned for, and got a part with, the national touring company for the smash hit, The Music Man, with Forrest Tucker. Jeff played one of the town's children, singing and dancing and displaying his natural talent and charisma.

The boy had good looks, as did Gaby, Frankie and Billy, too. It was no wonder. Mother Shirley was a beautiful blonde, and their father, Francis, was six-foot two, with dark hair and movie star looks. Francis and Shirley were second cousins who had never met until Francis had sought her out during a visit to L.A. on Navy leave in 1943. He had heard from his family that he had a relation from Yakima, Washington that had moved to Los Angeles. She was seven years his senior but that did nothing to blunt the instant attraction between them. They married the next year, on June 11, 1944.

Francis was from Chicago and had joined the Navy at seventeen, instantly finding himself in WWII and serving much of his time in the Aleutian Islands off the Alaskan coast, unloading ships and building bases as a Seabee. Both the United States and Japan, understanding the strategic importance of Alaska and the Aleutians, took action to secure the region for their respective sides; the Japanese had taken up military occupation of Attu and Kiska Islands, part of the Aleutians, and were ultimately defeated and driven out by the United States Army, Navy, and Air Force.

Shirley worked by day for the Army on a deciphering project, then volunteered evenings at the Hollywood USO, serving meals to servicemen.

At the war's end, Francis found himself with little qualifications for a professional career, so he bounced through a series of sales jobs, the kind that always sought applicants willing to work for commissions with anecdotal evidence of the fortunes to be made, no experience necessary. He took part-time work doing more menial things with guaranteed income until his ship came in on a sales job. With their fourth child, Gaby, being born in 1953, and a wife who worked at raising them, Francis was more than happy to suddenly discover the sort of income potential his own children apparently possessed.

It was an easier time for the DesEnfants family with the income of Jeff and Gaby. But then the family split up for a time as The Music Man left L.A. and began touring, including limited engagements in Dallas, San Francisco and Detroit. Francis and the two oldest boys Frankie and Billy stayed behind in L.A. while Shirley accompanied Jeff and elected to take Gaby, too, after getting an "okay" from the touring company. The company traveled by train and Shirley had to make her sleeper berth for two work for the three of them. The company provided a tutor for Jeff and the show's other children who all worked on commensurate curriculum. Gaby simply went without any schooling for a while, though she took dance lessons and worked at learning to read. Then the show settled at Chicago's Shubert Theatre for a thirteen month run. The family was reunited for a bit before older brothers Frankie and Billy went back to L.A. to live with their grandmother, Stella, affectionately known as Tedda. She was Shirley's mother and was happy to dote over her grand boys. Francis stayed in Chicago with Shirley, Jeff and Gaby. He was back in his hometown.

As Jeff worked his steady gig with The Music Man, Gaby landed regular work doing television commercials. She did spots for, Ipana Toothpaste; Campbell's Soup; Elgin Watch; Calgon Fabric Softener; Little Lady Cosmetics; Ball Jars; Mrs. Baird's Bread, and others. The money was steady and good. Francis and Shirley acted as facilitators and handlers; foregoing jobs themselves to make sure Jeff and Gaby were where they were supposed to be, when they supposed to be there.

Jeff was making two hundred a week which was paid each Friday in cash in a brown envelope. Francis was there each week to collect his son's wages, and being a regular backstage attendee at the shows, he came to know the employees and the culture. That culture included gambling at cards when there was a break in the action. The orchestra pit emptied into the Shubert's basement where tables quickly filled with musicians, some of whom delighted in a couple of quick hands of poker during the intermission of the show. Francis was a regular in the poker games and could schmooze with the best of them. "Let's go boys! The cards are hot and little time we got," he would call as the players hustled to their seats.

The national company's last show finally came to pass. For the last time, Francis and Jeff walked out the stage door that fed into an alley. They strolled up it towards the street as Francis held his son's hand. Turning the corner, Francis and Jeff walked under the marquee of the Shubert Theatre. Then, just beyond it, Francis suddenly stopped and turned, gazing back at the marquee with remembrance of all that it had meant over the past year of their lives. He stood looking, melancholy with the finality of it.

Jeff tugged on his father's hand. "Come on, dad, don't look back," he said.

Francis turned his eyes to his nine-year old son, knowing his boy had not an inkling of the profundity in the words he had just spoken, as if a mere instrument of the revelation he had just delivered. Francis's eyes welled with emotion.

"Right you are, son. No sense in it now. On we go."

Francis gripped his son's hand a little tighter as they continued up the street toward home and an uncertain future.

# 4

Shirley was always networking for Jeff and Gaby. Good luck came of her efforts just as Jeff's employment with The Music Man came to an end in Chicago. The mother of one of the other boys in the Chicago show told Shirley that the Broadway production of The Music Man, now starring Bert Parks, was about to hold auditions for the part of Amaryllis, and that little Gaby might be perfect for it. The part of Amaryllis included dialogue and dancing and an easily trainable bit of piano playing. Gaby's resume of television commercials was enough to get her an audition, and she landed the part.

Off to New York City they all went, with brothers Frankie and Billy reuniting to make the family whole again. They arrived by car at night in the midst of a blackout that gripped Manhattan for thirteen hours in August, 1959. The darkness was hot and humid with no streetlights, no traffic lights, and Francis having mostly no idea of where he was driving as they fought their way uptown in traffic that brought to mind the phrase, 'May the best man win'.

"Hey buddy," Francis yelled out the car window to an adjacent motorist, "Will I hit Amsterdam Street if I keep on this way?"

The man glared at him, irritated, and saw the six faces from the packed car looking hopefully at him. "Yeah, Mack…about noon tomorrow at this rate!"

An hour later, Francis knocked on the door of the landlord and got the key to a basement apartment under a bakery. "You got a flashlight?" the landlord asked. "It'll be pitch black down there."

"No…no flashlight," Francis replied.

"Hold on a minute," the landlord said before disappearing back inside his place. A moment later he returned. "Here," he said, handing Francis two candles and some matches. "This will help for a little bit, but you better get down to the corner store and get some more. Nobody knows how long this damn thing's gonna last. I'd go fast. If they're not out of candles yet, they will be soon."

After moving their luggage into their cramped apartment, they spent several hours on the stoop outside to escape the stifling heat of their new home. Sitting together, they ate sandwiches and watched people go by as they listened to the sounds of the night, which included a few screams and a gunshot or two. The power came on the next morning. The family huddled around the radio in their apartment and scanned the dial, stopping when they heard the deep voice say, "Coming to you from high atop the Ansonia Hotel." As it turned out, the Ansonia Hotel was only a few blocks from where they lived. The Ansonia's broadcasts of news and local shows would become a staple that provided entertainment and flavor of the resident culture.

Francis and Shirley had no money their first two days in New York as they awaited the arrival of Jeff's final pay from Chicago. The wonderful smells from the bakery upstairs added to the hunger they all endured before the money finally came. Then they indulged in a bakery feast of éclairs and cinnamon rolls just to get even.

A day later, Shirley and Gaby rode the subway for the first time on their way to the Majestic Theatre where Gaby would be working. The subway train was full with no seats available, so Shirley stood grasping a handrail with one hand while holding Gaby's hand with her other. None of the men bothered with offering their seat. A trio of Puerto Rican teenage girls soon boarded and stood near Shirley and Gaby. The girls began roughhousing, and one girl subsequently bumped into Shirley. A moment later, the girl was pushed by another and bumped hard into Shirley again. The sweetest of people by nature, Shirley politely asked her if she could refrain from running into her, as she was with her young daughter. The Puerto Rican girl who had bumped

*So Too My Love*

Shirley looked incredulous for a moment then punched Shirley in the face and told her to "shut up". The girls laughed and exited at the next stop as Shirley stood stoically with tears streaming down her face. A seated man full of bravado and courage looked up at Shirley and said, "Welcome to New York, Lady."

The family adapted to the rough and tumble of Manhattan; multitudes crammed together like an infestation in pursuit of survival before civility. The children all attended public schools in the neighborhood. Oldest brother, Frankie, started high school and gravitated to the greaser crowd, spending his free time roaming the streets and chasing skirts. Billy was much more reserved and introspective, keeping to himself and inwardly struggling with his adolescence as the upheaval and nomadic traits of his family weighed heavy on his sense of identity. Jeff enjoyed public school for a change and went to auditions and modeling jobs; there was no sign of a paper route in his immediate future. Gaby attended public school half-days and performed as Amaryllis in the evenings. She came to understand the teamwork necessary to the success of the show, reveling in the camaraderie of the cast as the show continued its long run, and eventually moved to the Broadway Theatre before its 1,375 consecutive New York performances came to an end in April, 1961.

Early in 1960, Jeff landed a part in the musical 'Gypsy', starring Ethel Merman. With Gaby and Jeff both working in Broadway shows, the money was good and the family enjoyed easier times once again. But the show ran its course and Gypsy ended its Broadway run in March, 1961, only a month before Gaby's work with The Music Man ended. Jeff continued on briefly with the touring company of Gypsy, still with Ethel Merman. The show played Rochester, New York, until early December whereupon it quite suddenly ended and the lights fell dark.

After Gaby appeared on Sing Along With Mitch and The Jackie Gleason Show, the work seemed to dry up. Francis and Shirley decided that any slim employment prospects for Gaby and Jeff failed to outweigh their desire to leave New York. The family was back in Los Angeles by the beginning of 1962.

They moved to Wilcox Avenue, a few blocks north of Hollywood Boulevard, in Hollywood. Their new home was a bungalow situated on a small courtyard across which Shirley's mother, Stella, AKA Tedda, and grandmother, Louise, lived.

Frankie, Billy, Jeff, and Gaby were enchanted to have their grandmother and great grandmother living so close. Great grandmother Louise was mostly bedridden but fawned over her great grandchildren whenever they stopped in, telling them stories of the old days, dispensing loving advice, and handing out quarters to go and have fun with. And grandmother Tedda baked cookies and cakes for them, and served as a confidant for any earthly problems. Great grandmother Louise went on to live 93 years.

While the older boys went to Hollywood High School, Jeff began junior high school at Le Conte, and Gaby attended Selma Elementary School. Jeff's acting and modeling career came to a standstill, and his interests turned to sports. He playing Little League Baseball and participated on all the school sports teams at Le Conte.

Gaby continued to work for another two years, primarily doing television series in brief episodic parts. She appeared in Wagon Train, Combat, McHale's Navy, The Phil Silvers Show, Wells Fargo, The Red Skelton Hour, and others. She also spent two days working in Bodega Bay, California as one of the terrorized school children running from a bird attack in the movie 'The Birds'. And she continued her stage work in summer stock productions of 'A Tree Grows in Brooklyn', and 'Gypsy'. Despite excellent reviews of her work, the well ran dry on work, and she settled back into a more normal childhood. Her father went back to sales jobs and whatever else he could find. It was a retreat to the struggle. Frankie and Billy both had their own jobs to have spending money. Jeff got a paper route.

# 5

Franklin was an imaginative boy, but he couldn't understand how those voices and music came out of box with the dial. And the bigger box, the new one they called the television, had people and things happening on the screen. How was that so? For days, whenever each was on, he would peer into the back or sides or wherever he might catch any glimpse of the inside, hoping to see the miniature people which he was sure lived in the devices. And horses, too; he had seen some on the screen. He even looked in when the radio or television were turned off, thinking maybe he would see the little people asleep in the back.

"Franklin, why are you still looking in there?" his mother asked one day as she saw him examining the television once again. "I told you there are no little people inside, Babe. The pictures and sound come over the airwaves. I know you don't understand airwaves, but it means there aren't any people in there. Understand?"

Franklin wasn't having any of it. He didn't understand airwaves but he understood Santa Claus. In a world where a man flew a sled and reindeer all over the world in one night, going up and down chimneys even if you didn't have one, Franklin was sure there could be tiny people in those boxes. Mom just didn't know about them. He did. He would find them, and then he would show her and she would know, too.

In 1958, a year after the mud fight at their house on Windsor, Franklin's family moved a few miles to a house at 135 N. Beachwood, just a half block south of Beverly Boulevard, and two blocks east of Larchmont Boulevard. A small, one-story house with a detached one-car garage and an incinerator in the backyard for burning trash, it was comfortable and resided in a nice, clean neighborhood. Two big pines trees stood in the front yard right across the street; perfect for climbing and overseeing all that was happening on the block.

Summertime had arrived. Franklin would turn six in September. His brother, Brian was eight, and sister, Marcia, the oldest, would turn eleven in August. Their mother, Nancy, was in her last year of law school at UCLA. The daughter of Frank Belcher, a famous trial lawyer and former California Bar Association President, Nancy had graduated from Stanford a dozen years earlier with a degree in English Literature. Starting law school at twenty-nine years old had materialized as her plan when it became clear that her husband, and father of their children, Harbert, could not hold a steady job due to his sour temperament and unchecked volatility.

Harbert grew up in Hailey, Idaho. The son of a sheep farmer, Harbert's life had been one misfortune after another. His mother died when he was seven, his father when he was fourteen. He lived with his father's sister, Aunt Hattie, through his high school years then enlisted in the Army after local opportunities failed to pan out to his desire. He ended up in the European theatre of WWII, fighting at the Battle of the Bulge as part of a three-man, fifty caliber machine gun crew. A German mortar shell exploded near him and seriously mangled his leg. He lost half of his right foot to the ensuing gangrene and sustained enough tissue loss in his thigh that his scar was several inches wide and deep, running from his hip to his knee. He was awarded a Purple Heart and discharged from the army, soon thereafter returning to Idaho where he took a wife. They had been married three weeks when she tragically died after tripping and tumbling down a flight of stairs. Devastated, Harbert left Idaho and briefly took advantage of the GI Bill, attending Stanford University just long enough to meet Nancy May Belcher.

*So Too My Love*

In an era when having sexual relations with someone meant likely betrothal, Nancy dutifully accepted Harbert's quick proposal of marriage, not yet knowing how emotionally and psychologically crippled he was. Nancy's father sized Harbert up fairly early on. His new son-in-law was very bright and could be charming when he wanted, but he seemed skittish and could turn mean in a blink. Harbert would dwell in the shadow of Nancy's very successful and powerful father, a man who had every idea that his daughter had made a mistake. Harbert's own sense of inadequacy drove his growing resentment toward his father-in-law, and by association, Nancy too. That Harbert had two young sons who injected their own brand of misfit strife into the family circumstances did not help.

The morning's coolness had waned as five-year old Franklin sat on a neighbor's lawn looking at the book of matches he had recently lifted from somewhere. He was considering the power of his new possession when Brian happened along.

"I got some matches," he said to his brother as if he had a magic lamp with a genie inside.

"Let's burn somethin'," Brian immediately replied.

After scouting the neighborhood for a brief time, the target of opportunity appeared like a riptide, pulling them into a sea of inconsequence and abandonment of what infinitesimal rational thought each seldom had. From the sidewalk they could see the firewood piled along the wall of the garage, its door open. After glancing about to see that no one was watching, they scampered up the driveway and into the garage located only half a block away from their own house. To add to the misalignment of the stars, a plainly marked can of kerosene sat directly next to the wood pile. It proved to be a breathtaking catalyst. Flames jumped from the woodpile with a ferocity that shocked them both, causing them to run from the garage with a rush of fear that fully contradicted any previously imagined thrill. Franklin jumped up and seated himself on the handlebars and Brian began pedaling his bike with the surge of adrenaline.

They rode around the block, scared the entire time of what they might see when they passed again. As the garage came back into view, it was completely engulfed in flames, a sight which sent shivers through Franklin and dropped his stomach as if he'd leapt from the top of a building. Several neighbors stood out in front of their homes, awestruck by the fire. Brian pedaled right on by and kept going.

The garage burnt to the ground taking everything in it, including a new Cadillac. Fortunately, it had been a detached garage, and the quick response of the fire department kept anything else from going up. Nobody had seen anything, so a fire investigator began door to door inquiries. Sister Marcia was already in the know, having been confided in by her two scared shitless brothers. She saw the investigator working his way around the neighborhood, so she and Brian began coaching Franklin about what to say and how to deny knowing anything about what had happened. It might have worked out if the fire investigator had spoken to them as a group. Instead, he conducted the interviews separately, and Franklin was a wreck once his turn came. When Franklin stood in front of the towering investigator with only his mother present, he didn't stand a chance.

"Do you know anything about how the fire started?" the investigator asked, his voice deep and suspicious, and his searing gaze burning through any planned veil of deception.

Franklin stood frozen for a moment, and then he cracked. His eyes filled with tears. "We didn't mean to do it," he blubbered.

Brian received several rounds of whippings and was grounded for the rest of the summer. For spilling his guts, Franklin somehow escaped the whippings but was also grounded. The older couple whose garage had been burnt down refused to press any charges and would not accept any payment for their losses, graciously insisting that their insurance would cover everything.

The severity of his offense was not lost on Franklin. For a long time after, he promoted no more malice than throwing a dirt clod or two, and sometimes arrived home late, the day's play and adventure being beyond any comprehension of time. But the phrase 'spare the rod, spoil the child', seemed as the looming rationale for the increasingly irrational infliction of punishment by his father, Harbert, who appeared to take pleasure in the dispensing of it. At the time, it was not an unusual practice in many American homes for children to be spanked with a belt, which happened to be the instrument of choice for Harbert. What was unusual for Franklin and Brian was the duration of each episode, the perceived infraction that brought about the whipping, and what end of the belt they might receive.

On one occasion, Harbert whipped Franklin soundly for having dropped a piece of cake on the floor. The cotton pajamas Franklin wore did little to mitigate the force of the lashing. Franklin's mother, Nancy, used a washcloth and bowl of warm water to clean the bleeding welts on his back, buttocks and legs. Franklin was most taken with the tears that rolled down his mother's face as she tended to him, not knowing that her tears came at the realization of what kind of man she had married and what he might be capable of. For his part, Harbert liked to preface his whippings with fear inducing statements. "I got a little present for you," was a favorite, especially when Nancy wasn't around, which was often because she worked and attended classes in pursuit of her law degree.

As the only woman in her class, Nancy graduated from UCLA law school in 1959 and soon thereafter went to work as a licensed attorney in her father's law firm of Belcher, Henzie & Biegenzahn. About the same time, the family moved to a house at 828 South Longwood. It was a big house on a nice street. The back yard was huge and had a stream populated with crawdads that ran through it. Franklin felt like he'd moved to Tom Sawyer's island. He spent hours down at the stream, playing in the thick brush around it and catching crawdads from the water with a piece of string baited with whatever morsel was handy. On occasion, Franklin would see a Japanese man catching crawdads at the stream of the next-door neighbor. Franklin soon learned that the man was the gardener, and he caught crawdads to take home and eat. Franklin preferred to just play with them, but soon endeavored to put them into orbit taped aboard a soup can with a firecracker halfway inserted in a top-drilled hole. The can would be placed in a larger base can; usually a tuna can, with a half inch of water in it. When the implanted firecracker exploded, the pressure would launch the soup can between fifty and a hundred feet into the air. Many a crawdad rode the rocket.

Franklin's happiest times as a child occurred when the family loaded up in the station wagon and headed for Hailey, Idaho, to visit Aunt Hattie in Harbert's home town. While living on Longwood, they made the trip two years in a row as a summertime vacation. They left Los Angeles late at night to cross the Mojave Desert at its coolest, carrying a canvas water bag strapped to the front grill of the car in case of overheating.

It was a grand adventure. With the second seat folded down, Marcia, Brian, and Franklin had blankets and pillows laid out in back along with a stash of candy and a good supply of comic books which always included favorites like Superman, Captain America, Archie, Betty and Veronica, Jughead, Richie Rich, Hot Stuff the Little Devil, and a host of others. Off into the night they would go, reading comic books by flashlight until sleep finally overtook them. Then they would come awake as they reached Las Vegas shortly before dawn. The brilliant oasis of lights in the middle of the desert lit the night sky as if they'd reached the Kingdom of Oz. The stop there would be short but always yielded a few silver dollars for the children. They were bigger and heavier than any coins they'd ever seen. It seemed Las Vegas must be the only place in the world that had them, a notion which added to the magic of the journey.

From Las Vegas they drove straight north on Highway 93, a route they eventually named 'slaughter alley' because of the incredible number of rabbits that got run over on the highway. The carnage looked like a war zone; blood and fur splattered and smeared on the road with a frequency of several per mile. Their own car produced endless thumps as it unavoidably hit its share of new rabbits running onto the highway. There was no telling if nuclear detonations at the nearby Nevada Proving Grounds had caused some sort of explosion of the rabbit population, or if the tests had just driven every rabbit in Nevada to Highway 93. It was beyond freakish.

Hailey was a small, quiet town, so far removed from Los Angeles in every manner that it seemed like a trip back in time. Aunt Hattie lived on the main street in a quaint little house with a giant elm tree in the front yard. The cuckoo clock in the parlor room was the only one Franklin had ever seen. He soon came to understand the quarter hour chimes and the cuckoo's appearance on the hour, spellbound as the birdhouse door opened and the cuckoo came forth to deliver its song before retreating back inside. In the kitchen, Aunt Hattie cooked on a four plate woodstove with an oven below, another complete novelty to the children who were always eager to help clean the ashes and load the new wood. And she could cook like nobody's business. A short and stout woman, Aunt Hattie herself was as nice as if she had come from a fairy tale, her sweet demeanor and loving treatment always inspiring the children's best behavior. Even Harbert watched himself around her, putting his bad ways aside during their stay.

Aunt Hattie took them fishing at beautiful forest streams where she taught her secrets and demonstrated her own extraordinary fishing prowess, reeling in twenty-inch trout like the Pied Piper. She could fry them up even better than she could catch them. Franklin couldn't imagine anything that tasted better than Aunt Hattie's trout.

Marcia, Brian, and Franklin reveled in all of it; fishing, catching grasshoppers, getting a Coca Cola for a dime down at the filling station, or getting to shoot the .22 rifle in the country, and even drive the car on dirt roads. And they went to the Ketchum pool, just a few miles from Hailey. The pool had a fourteen-foot deep end and a small platform called the 'crow's nest' that was perched a lofty thirty feet above the water. Watching the daring ones climb up the ladder was enough to make Franklin quiver. He was content just to swim and work at performing front and back flips off the diving board.

The week-long trips to Hailey were the best of times and always seemed to end too soon.

# 6

When the movie West Side Story came out in 1961, Franklin was enthralled by the brilliance of the music and dancing. He managed to get the album and played it over and over, listening as the black vinyl disc spun its contents, the orchestra delivering abstract primal melodies and rhythm like nothing he'd ever heard before, moving him in ways he'd never felt before. And the dancing in the movie was sensational to him. For weeks he danced around the neighborhood recreating his own version of the Jets and the Sharks. His new obsession did not go unnoticed by his parents. Nancy offered him the chance to take modern jazz dance instruction at Panieff Ballet Studio on La Brea a few blocks north of Wilshire. Franklin jumped at the offer and began attending class once a week, learning moves and routines which he would practice between classes. His instructor told Nancy that Franklin showed promise and had natural athletic ability with a good sense of rhythm. The instructor also noted Franklin's size for his age, speculating that he would likely end up too big to imagine dancing as a profession one day. Franklin began to be teased by friends about taking dance lessons and going to a dance studio which had 'ballet' in its title, so before long he gave it up.

He soon replaced his dance interests with an after-school job selling the L.A. Herald to southbound motorists at the corner of Highland and Wilshire. Franklin stood on the center median strip of Highland each day from 4:00 to 6:00P.M., calling out the headlines to south-bounders stopped at the red light. He became fast at getting to those who signaled him, making change from his apron pouch with the ease and speed of a successful junior businessman. "Get your paper here!" he would yell, moving up and down the line of cars for maximum visibility. He loved it, and loved the money he made. Upon his next report card coming out, Franklin received a sound whipping and was forced to quit his job. His grades never did improve.

In 1962, Franklin relinquished his status of youngest sibling when newest baby sister Diane was born from an unplanned pregnancy. With Nancy being the breadwinner, Harbert became a stay-at-home dad, aided by Marcia, Brian, Franklin, and a few different part-time nannies, each of whom eventually quit due to Harbert's abusive treatment. Marcia, Brian and Franklin were equally unhappy about their father being around all the time. When Harbert moved through the house, his slippers made a distinctive sound of 'shh shh shh shh' as he shuffled about, not lifting his feet. Hearing his slippers shuffling over to the bottom of the stairs would likely be followed by a command. "Come on down here, Franklin, I've got a little present for you." Those were the words which Franklin feared hearing, for he had heard them so many times. And Brian heard his name called with equal frequency. The whippings and beatings mostly occurred when Nancy was not home, and were most often followed by a warning from Harbert. "If you tell your mother, I'll kill you," he would say. Marcia ordinarily remained above the fray. She was a good student and stayed out of trouble, but every once in a while even she faced his sadistic side.

Harbert had always been verbally abusive to Nancy, and the children had witnessed him slapping her on several occasions. Over time, Harbert's physical abuse of Nancy began to escalate, particularly when she attempted to intervene on behalf of Franklin or Brian when either faced an imminent whipping in her presence. Then it was Nancy who got slapped, punched or whipped. Nancy mysteriously turned up with a ruptured spleen that required emergency surgery. The children did not connect the dots at the time as Nancy blamed it on an accidental fall.

*So Too My Love*

Brian and Franklin began plotting as to how they could kill their father, speaking in low whispers as they lay in their beds at night. They talked of shooting him, or stabbing him as he slept. They talked of poisoning him. But, the talks usually ended with acknowledgment that he would kill them if their attempt was unsuccessful. They lived in fear and loathing of him, but it would not be for much longer.

Nancy suffered the embarrassment and shame of her failed marriage. It was her drive to succeed at everything she undertook that held her captive in her marriage for better than sixteen years. But, enough was enough. She decided to end it. In the summer of 1964, Nancy had Harbert served with divorce papers. Shocked, Harbert told her she would never live to see it through, threatening that he would have her in the sights of a rifle before it ever came to pass. Nancy informed the police of her intentions and of Harbert's threat. Harbert denied the threat to the police, nevertheless a restraining order was issued and Harbert was forced to move out. Harbert continued to call her at home and at work to threaten her life. Nancy's father, Frank, hired an armed bodyguard for his daughter. The guard stayed at the house. In a very tumultuous few days, all pretenses had ended. Nancy was determined to be rid of Harbert.

Franklin was away at Camp Whittle in the San Bernardino Mountains when the end arrived. His grandfather had arranged the two week experience for him, perhaps knowing it would be an opportune time for him to be elsewhere. Franklin received the news of his parent's pending divorce, and the departure of his father, when his mother and siblings came to collect him at the end of the camp session.

"You mean he's not living at our house anymore?" Franklin asked with the deepest hope. "He's gone?"

"He sure is," Brian gleefully exclaimed "There's a guy named Robert staying at our house in case Dad comes around. Robert's got a gun. He'll plug Dad if he tries anything."

In one instant, the weight of the world had been lifted from Franklin's shoulders, making the occasion the happiest day of his young life. Two months later, Franklin started junior high at John Burroughs Junior High School as a B-7. Brian was an A-9 and would graduate from John Burroughs in January. Marcia started her senior year at Los Angeles High School. L.A. High School had diverse demographics in its student population, and they had a great football team that won the City Championship that year. In an era before political correctness, kids in Los Angeles existed together with little concern of race and racism. A popular cheer from the L.A. High School stands during a football game went like this: "Buddaheads, Spooks, Greyboys, Jews, with that combination how can you lose!"

Nancy wanted to move, to get a fresh start away from Harbert and the house they had shared. In October, 1964, she took her four children and moved north several miles to Hollywood. Their new home sat at 1905 North Curson Drive, between La Brea and Laurel Canyon, and one long block north of Hollywood Boulevard. Marcia wanted to finish her senior year at L.A. High, so she commuted each day in an old Rambler. Brian had only two months to go before his mid-year graduation from John Burroughs Junior High, so he commuted with Marcia. He would start Hollywood High School in January, 1965. Franklin transferred from John Burroughs to Le Conte Junior High School, in whose district they now resided. He rode the school bus and was happy for a new start in a new neighborhood

From Hollywood Boulevard, northbound Curson Drive was a long, straight street running uphill nearly a third of a mile before reaching a circular intersection where their house resided at the corner of Curson and Curson Terrace. Curson continued on up another mile, eventually winding back southwest before dead-ending at an isolated spot known as 'The Point'. The view of the city from The Point was particularly impressive. On a clear day, you could see to the ocean. At night, the city lights twinkled below, rolling out to the end of visibility. Those who knew about The Point dropped in for a little of this and a little of that, mostly underage drinking or making out.

At twelve years old, Franklin was taken with the adventure of living in the Hollywood hills. From the top of Curson, he rode his homemade skateboard down the long hill, traversing back and forth in a way that made one trip down last for half an hour. He also loved riding his skateboard on the smooth, marble-like surface of Hollywood Boulevard, taking in all the stars names as he slalomed around them like racing gates.

Franklin soon discovered a big time could be had in an old wagon. He would roll out of their garage in a Red Flyer wagon, picking up speed through the intersection then hitting the straightaway down Curson and speeding straight down the hill at near thirty miles per hour until the bailout point of Wattles driveway where the gentle turn into the parallel driveway was akin to hitting a runaway truck ramp.

For the first year or so on Curson, Nancy leased out the bottom floor of their house. It was small and completely separate from the rest of the house and had its own entrance. The tenant, Fred Roos, seemed a nice man of about thirty years of age. He came and went each day in an old Mercedes, always offering up a cordial 'hello' whenever he happened to cross paths with any of the family. Franklin tried not to stare when Fred would roll up with some beautiful girl, which Franklin noted happened quite often. Franklin began to observe Fred with one particular girl much more and figured he now had a girlfriend. Unknown to Franklin at the time, Fred was a casting director for a number of television shows. Fred eventually moved out and up, becoming a producer and winning an Oscar for 'The Godfather II, along with the rest of the Coppola gang.

School proved much more of a challenge to Franklin than gaining an education. He was troublesome, obstinate, and defiant, and lacked many skills and any confidence. He could read well only because he had read a lot, immensely enjoying the escapism of a good story. But he did little of his work, caring not of the consequences. Elementary school had been a terrible struggle and he entered junior high school with little academic foundation. When his father had left, Franklin had consciously vowed that he would not take grief from anyone, other than his mother, ever again. His residual anger ran deep, permeating him in ways he did not understand and could not control. As troubled youth so often live only in the here and now, with no regard for the future or the effect of present actions upon it, Franklin was adrift with hate. It would not serve him well. After ignoring his schoolwork, and repeated episodes of disrespect to his teachers, he was expelled from Le Conte Junior High School near the end of his seventh grade school year. His next stop, Bancroft Junior High School, soon produced more of the same. He got into several fights and demonstrated complete disrespect to authority. After several suspensions, his expulsion from Bancroft came at the end of the school year when he was informed that he would not be accepted back for the eighth grade.

As the summer of 1965 arrived, Franklin developed a burning interest in drums. His mother had a burning interest in seeing him pursue anything constructive, so she helped him procure his first kit, a five piece set of St. George Drums. Declining the offer of lessons, Franklin spent hours playing and became self-taught, demonstrating natural ability and exercising a work-ethic of practice that brought rapid improvement.

In August, The Beatles came to town to play a show at the Hollywood Bowl. Franklin, Brian, Marcia, Nancy and everyone else who lived on Curson couldn't believe it when The Beatles moved into a house just up the street on Curson Terrace for several days before their show. Overnight, their location became known and police barricades went up on Curson just below where Franklin's house sat on the corner of Curson and Curson Terrace. No one could get past the barricades without showing proof of living beyond them. Not having a driver's license yet, Franklin carried a copy of the electric bill with him. From his house, he could see the throngs of people, mostly girls, at the barricades only several hundred feet away. One day he opened the windows and put a Beatles album on the powerful hi-fi, then began playing his drums. The drums gave just enough of a live effect that the barricade crowd imagined The Beatles were practicing. Franklin could hear the screams from outside over his own playing. But the pandemonium soon faded as the crowd eventually heard enough to know it wasn't real, other than the antics of a twelve-year old boy who had momentarily duped them.

From the back of Franklin's house he could climb the hillside and end up in the backyard bushes of the house where The Beatles were staying. One night he did it and watched from the bushes about fifty feet away as an outdoor party was in full swing. He saw John Lennon standing on a small bridge that spanned the figure-eight swimming pool at its narrowest point. Lennon began scratching his bum and Franklin laughed, imagining he had witnessed the story of the week, knowing that all the girls at the police barricades below would have paid good money to be in the catbird seat he now occupied.

# 7

In autumn, 1965, Franklin began the eighth grade at Ridgewood Military Academy, a private school on the west side of the San Fernando Valley. His grandfather thought Franklin would be best off in the structured environment of a boarding school; and Nancy needed a break from the grief Franklin caused with his public school expulsions. Franklin started out with a good attitude, attempting his schoolwork and keeping his mouth shut. He got to go home on weekends, leaving Friday afternoons and returning on Sunday evenings. At school, he spent much of his free time in the small band room. It had a drum set on which he could practice when the room wasn't in use. He managed to get in some time every day, finding solace in the kinetic expression and release which came from playing.

During the spring semester, Franklin joined the track team at the coach's urging. He took up the shot put. Seeing how far he could throw an iron ball seemed preferable to all the running the other kids did. He did well with the shot and set a new school record for his grade. For a while he became rather gangly and awkward, growing from five-foot seven inches to six feet tall and 150 pounds during the school year. Franklin had stayed out of fights and had not been overly disrespectful, nevertheless he did not do his school work and his grades reflected his failings. At the end of the school year, Ridgewood informed Nancy that her son would not be allowed to return.

For the 9th grade, Franklin attended Army-Navy Military Academy, a somewhat prestigious prep boarding school located right on the coast in Carlsbad, California. Nancy told Franklin to give his best effort because his grandfather had paid the expensive tuition and there would be no refund if Franklin were expelled.

Putting it in those terms impacted Franklin's thinking. He was determined to avoid expulsion. The year would be long for him as cadets were allowed to go home only one weekend a month, and for Thanksgiving and Christmas.

It did not take Franklin long to realize that Army-Navy Academy was principally a school for juvenile delinquents with wealthy parents or benefactors. All manner of shenanigans occurred. The school population, which began with over 400 cadets grades 9-12, whittled away week by week, month by month. Who had been booted out each week became a regular topic of discussion amongst those who remained. The FBI showed up once after someone had thrown a piece of pipe at the train that ran along the east side of the football field. It was a revelation for all that throwing things at a moving train is a federal offense.

Army-Navy Academy had a ninth grade football team which played a seven game schedule against other schools. The coach asked Franklin if he wanted to play, so he joined up. The first day of practice was an ordeal just trying to get out of the locker room. He had never put on a real football uniform before. Inserting his left and right thigh pads and knee pads properly into the respective sleeves of his football pants was like an IQ test. Then he had to figure out those damn hip pads and tail pad, not to mention the shoulder pads and trying to get his jersey on over them. The helmet weighed enough to kill somebody with.

Once he got on the field the practices were exciting, though Franklin had little grasp of what he was supposed to be doing. He did, however, quickly discover that he liked to run into people. It seemed he couldn't get hurt with all that stuff on. But then he learned he could get the crap knocked out of him if he wasn't paying attention. He started paying more attention. When the first game arrived, Franklin went in at defensive tackle. He lined up in the right spot but his nerves and adrenaline seemed to erase his entire thought process as he awaited his first play in a football game. At the snap of the ball, all turned to mad chaos as players ran every which way. He got hit from the front, the side, the back, and he was sure somebody tried to drop a Kansas farmhouse on his head. He was immediately pulled from the game. His coach was waiting for him when he reached the sideline.

"Did you forget what you were supposed to do?" the coach asked mildly. "You were supposed to slant to the A gap."

The coach's words struck sudden remembrance in Franklin who rolled his eyes. "Sorry coach, I forgot. I couldn't hardly think."

"It can happen," the coach said, his eyes expressing understanding. "All right, don't worry about slanting or anything else. I want you to do just one thing. Okay?"

"Sure coach, whadaya want me to do?"

The coach put his hands on Franklin's shoulder pads and looked him hard in the eye. "When the ball is snapped, I want you to run through their line and tackle whoever has the ball…got it? Follow the ball and tackle whoever has it as fast as you can…okay?"

Franklin nodded nervously fast. "Okay, coach."

"Now, what are you going to do?" the coach asked in immediate follow-up.

"I'm gonna follow the ball and tackle whoever has it."

The coach slapped his shoulder pads. "That's right! Run right through their line. The quarterback gets the snap first. Get him! If he hands it off, get the guy he hands it to. If he tries to throw a pass, get him before he can. Just follow the ball! Now get in there!"

The concept was simple to Franklin. He went back into the game and began wreaking havoc, making tackles all over the field and chasing the ball wherever it went. It was a singular focus and he just naturally played through whoever got in his way as he chased the ball. He got faked out a few times but steadily got better at recognizing the real handoffs from the fakes. He chased that ball.

*  *  *  *

    Franklin had found the band room not long after arriving at Army-Navy Academy. To his delight, there was a drum set that he could avail himself of. It wasn't long before word was out that he could play well. Some upperclassmen asked him to join their band; two guitars and an electric organ. Franklin joined them. A month later they played a school dance on campus that a nearby girls' school had been invited to. It was big stuff. Everybody loved the band, especially when they played 'Midnight Hour' and '96 Tears'.
    After the football season, Franklin went out for the ninth grade basketball team. They lost their first game 66 to 8. Franklin scored four of the eight points so he didn't feel as completely humiliated as he figured he should have. They never won a game that season. Franklin missed the last several games after he came down with a severe case of mononucleosis, which the doctor called, "The kissing disease." He remembered kissing a girl from the girls' school and figured her to be the reason for his present predicament.. The doctor quarantined Franklin to the school infirmary where he remained for a month, confined to his own room which at least had a window. His throat was so swollen he couldn't eat. For several days they had him hooked up to an I.V. and administered salt water treatments through his nose several times a day. He read a few books, did some school work, and stared out the window, watching cadets crossing the quad area between classes.
    Halfway through his month of quarantine, the nurse brought him a radio from her home. Franklin was extremely appreciative and happy, and adhered to her instructions about listening only at certain times. One day he heard the new Beatles song 'Strawberry Fields'. He initially thought the recording was warped but soon decided it was just something very different from every pop, rock, dance, blues, folk, jazz, or love song he'd ever heard before. The song played like a seminal

offering, completely groundbreaking as a clear line of demarcation where the 1960's spawned the psychedelic counterculture for which the decade would become infamously known.

When Franklin finally left the infirmary, he was six foot, one inch tall and weighed 147 pounds. It was the end of February, 1967. He had been home twice since the school year began, at Thanksgiving and Christmas. He would not go home again anytime soon.

Though Franklin refrained from any serious transgressions, his deficient school work and other numerous minor infractions brought about penalty hours of 'Extra Duty', a consequence in which the offender wore his regular uniform with the addition of leggings, a helmet, and a rifle, and then marched back and forth in front of the commandant's office. Franklin marched for two hours after school on weekdays, and then a minimum of two hours each on Saturdays and Sundays, with the option to complete more if he wanted to. Franklin knew he would be expelled if he refused to march, so he marched every day. He simply accumulated extra duty hours much faster than he could march them off. By the end of May, he had 351 hours of extra duty to complete. The school's commandant finally decided they'd had enough of Franklin, expelling him just weeks before the end of the school year. Nearly half of the school's cadets had already been expelled.

Franklin returned home to Hollywood. In a turn of luck, he was accepted back to Le Conte Junior High School, the same school he had been expelled from as a seventh grader. He finished the three remaining weeks in Le Conte's semester. In an act of mercy, or perhaps just good riddance, Franklin was allowed to graduate. He would begin Hollywood High School in the fall.

# 8

The summer of 1967 unfolded as an experiment in boundaries for Franklin. He lived at home again on a virtually unsupervised basis. Nancy worked full time, and the live-in housekeeper/nanny, Lucilla, from Guadalajara, spoke little English and looked after baby sister Diane who was five-years old. Marcia and Brian had jobs and did their own thing, and hung out with their own friends. Franklin landed a part-time day job at Hollywood Liquor, a liquor store on the corner of Hollywood and La Brea. He cleaned up, stocked the cooler and shelves, and whatever else the owner wanted. When not at work, Franklin was generally out of control.

Early in the summer, Franklin smoked pot for the first time then spent the rest of the summer trying to get more. It was hard to come by, particularly for a fourteen-year old, and he didn't have much money. He pestered friends whom he knew might be holding and managed to get a joint here and a joint there, the insidious nature of his new obsession lost in the haze of the escapism. At night, he hitchhiked around, sometimes out Sunset Boulevard where he watched bands at Gazzarri's, or sometimes up Laurel Canyon where he hung out at The Store in hopes of scoring a little weed.

In July, the psychedelic rock band Jefferson Airplane came to L.A. to play some shows. They stayed at the same house where The Beatles had stayed, just up the hill from Franklin's house. The sprawling home at the top of Curson Terrace had been vacant for several years except for occasionally being rented by high profile folks. Unlike The Beatles' visit, no street barricades or heavy security existed for Jefferson Airplane's brief stay. Franklin climbed up the hill one night and walked out of the bushes into an empty yard. Live music emanated from the massive, knotty-pine sided house where scenes of the movie Point Blank, with Lee Marvin, had recently been filmed. Franklin walked directly into the cavernous room which had little furniture. Several rotating colored strobe lights dimly lit the darkened room, giving the appearance of an underground nightclub. Jefferson Airplane was playing at one end of the room as nearly a hundred people watched, some dancing off to the sides while others sat on the floor up close to the band. A pungent cloud of weed blanketed the room.

Nobody had noticed or cared when Franklin entered the room from a side door. He moved to the back and watched as Grace Slick crooned on in some long, weird trance of a song that Franklin had never heard before. Franklin spotted the half a joint in an ashtray on a small table and immediately grabbed it. He lit it and smoked away, noticing that it was stronger and a bit different in aroma than anything he'd ever smoked before. Keeping it for himself, Franklin didn't bother offering any nearby attendees a hit and just smoked away until he could no longer hold the tiny roach, his fingers toasted from the attempt. Soon the colored strobe lights became more interesting than the band, and that was all he remembered.

The sun had risen new to the day when Franklin sluggishly awakened, his reemergence of senses creeping on like one who'd been down the rabbit hole in pursuit of white rabbits. He opened his eyes and sat up. The room sat empty of everyone but himself. He couldn't believe it. No other bodies anywhere, just trash and remnants of the private party. Franklin got to his feet and listened to the silence. He walked to the front of the room where the band's equipment still resided. Franklin examined the drum set that Spencer Dryden had been playing the night before. *Wow, this is a bitchen set*, he thought. The strap on Franklin's own bass drum pedal had recently broken. In half a minute more he had the pedal from Dryden's set unfastened and headed for the door. No signs of life were present as Franklin left the way he had come, making his way back into the bushes before descending the hillside and returning home with his new pedal. He felt a moment of guilt for having stolen it, right up until he had the pedal affixed to his own kick drum. There would be no more visits to the house on Curson Terrace. The Smothers Brothers bought it soon afterwards.

* * * *

"You better get your butt runnin'!" Brian said to his younger brother one morning. "Practice starts in less than a month. Hell week'll kick your ass if you're not ready. It'll kick your ass anyway, but you better show up ready."

"Yeah, I will," Franklin replied with substantial conviction. He was excited at the prospect of high school football, especially getting to play on the same team as his brother who would be a senior. In the midst of his bad habits and indulgences, Franklin had made it to the weight-room a few times a week. Working out was a bright spot in his life. He knew it. Now he was six-two and weighed 170 pounds. He had enough size to play on the varsity line like his brother, if he could make it.

Franklin attended his first summertime, non-mandatory informal field workout the next day. The workout took place at Le Conte Junior High School so as not to violate rules on when and where a school could practice. None of Hollywood's coaches were present. Instead, Le Conte's head P.E. teacher, Mr. Hills, conducted the workout, doing so at the behest of Lou Birnbaum, Hollywood High School's head football coach. Franklin felt like a big shot just being in the presence of some of the varsity players.

"Hello, Franklin," Mr. Hills genially said. "What position do you want to work at?"

"Can I try quarterback?" Franklin asked on a whim. He could throw a football well and figured he should give it a shot.

"Quarterback, eh?" Mr. Hills said with a hint of skepticism. "Not following in your brother's footsteps?"

"Well, maybe I will, but my brother's not here right now."

Mr. Hills nodded. "Okay, get on over with that group and wait your turn."

Franklin trotted over to where two quarterbacks and a group of receivers were running passing drills. For the first time, Franklin saw Jeff DesEnfants. Unbeknownst to Franklin, Jeff had a younger sister. Her name was Gaby.

"Nice throw, Jeff," the other quarterback said after Jeff threw a long ball and hit the receiver perfectly in stride.

Franklin stood watching as Jeff threw another half dozen passes to differing routes, each time hitting the receiver right on the money. Jeff was entering his junior year and was already the presumed starter, a fact Franklin didn't know about but would not have disputed after what he'd just seen. Jeff could throw the football.

"Go ahead, I've already been once" the other quarterback said to Franklin when Jeff stepped aside.

All eyes turned to Franklin as he stepped forward to take a rotation. The returning players at Hollywood certainly knew Franklin's brother, Brian, but recognized nothing of this incoming sophomore who looked, at least, physically formidable.

"Run some quick outs," Mr. Hills said to the receivers.

The next two minutes were an exercise in embarrassment as Franklin threw a half dozen passes in the dirt short of the receivers.

The analysis of his audition was quick and decisive. "Why don't you go over there and work with the lineman," Mr. Hills said in a tone that conveyed more than just a suggestion.

The die was cast.

# 9

Hell Week began at the end of August, so named because it was a week's worth of two-a-day practices which marked the official start of the 1967 football campaign for the Hollywood High Sheiks.

For Franklin, whose steady descent had picked up speed during the summer, football served as a lifeline. He stopped smoking weed and worked out hard for several weeks before the start of Hell Week. He wasn't in great shape and did not possess confidence, but he was determined to prove himself worthy and hard working. Franklin was intent on showing head coach Louis Birnbaum that he wanted to play.

A tough and brilliant man with a Ph.D. in history, Coach Birnbaum prevailed as naturally inspirational in manner and action. As dimwitted as Franklin was, he instinctively knew Lou Birnbaum to be a very special man and coach, and sensed honor in playing for him. Coach Birnbaum had played college ball at Utah back in the leather helmet days; his face had a few places where it appeared as if golfers had been practicing with sand wedges. A true academic, Birnbaum authored several scholarly works including, 'Red Dawn at Lexington', an exposition on the beginnings of the American Revolution'. He taught his history classes with narrative that played as storytelling, his profound expertise on the subject delivered in a most engaging and colorful way.

The first day of practice stood hot. The freshly mowed grass invaded Franklin's olfactory with the sense of the experience to come, its pungent regard as osmosis for an etched memory, like the spark of a song remembered serving up the emotion of a particular time. The smell of fresh cut grass would forever evoke memories of football in Franklin.

Horace Mumps came unknown to Franklin and looked like prime sausage encased in a body, his two-hundred thirty pounds packed on a frame of about six-feet. Horace looked imposing by size and ended up paired with Franklin for a live tackling drill in which they started from ten yards apart. Franklin would tackle first, with Horace acting as the running back.

"Don't hit me too hard and I won't hit you too hard either," Horace whispered across to Franklin as Coach Birnbaum steadily approached, watching each pairing. It was the first hitting drill, the first chance to make an impression on Coach Birnbaum. Franklin didn't bother responding to Horace; he'd get his chance to do that in just a few seconds more.

Coach stepped to where they waited their turn. "Set...go!" he barked out.

Horace started forward at a rather timid pace. Franklin shot forward for all he was worth, staring at the numbers on Horace's jersey just before he slammed them with his face. Horace's feet lifted from the turf as his body went horizontal and thumped the ground like he had fallen from the top of a ladder, the hard impact accompanied by an exhalation of the air leaving his body. Horace sucked for air, unable to get his breath for a moment.

"That's the way to strike through the man!" Coach Birnbaum declared approvingly.

"Go ahead and hit me as hard as you want," Franklin said quietly to Horace as he was getting off him, "'Cause I'm not slowing down for you."

A moment later it was Horace's turn to tackle Franklin. Franklin did his best to impersonate a fullback on fourth and one at the goal line, hitting Horace and bowling him over. Horace sought out another partner for all future tackling drills.

# 10

At the end of Hell Week, the Angelo brothers, one a senior, one a junior, both of them tough kids, hosted a football party at their house on a Sunday afternoon. All the coaches, players, and their families were invited. The Angelo house resided in the Los Feliz area, the home being opulent with a private front yard, complete with fountains and an array of visual delights in flora and native trees.

Franklin was excited to attend but soon felt out of sorts in such a setting. There seemed to be over a hundred people. His social immaturity in evidence to himself, he quickly migrated away from the crowds which congregated outside. The day had consented with beauty, and the yard had several buffet tables loaded with delectable dishes of meats, salads, desserts, and soft refreshments.

Franklin found his way into a parlor through double doors which stood open to the yard. The interior of the Spanish style house fascinated his eye with arches, high ceilings, and massive lathe walls adorned with elegant oil paintings and tapestries and artifacts. Bronzes and marble statues resided in varying spots about the room. In the corner of the parlor sat a grand piano. Franklin stood taking it all in, alone and gratified of it. He made his way to the piano and sat down.

After a few moments, he began to plink at the keys and try three and four note chords, every now and again bringing forth something harmonious, but only equal to the number of distressed sounds he also produced. The room was light and airy, cool with its spaciousness. Then, she appeared just inside the doors, her beauty instantly the focus of his complete but disguised attention. Her dark hair fell down and beyond her shoulders. Her blue eyes nonchalantly looked the room over and settled on Franklin who suddenly felt like an escaped convict caught in a searchlight. A woman walked in and stood next to her. She, too, gave Franklin the once over.

Shirley leaned in close to her daughter's ear. "That's a nice looking boy over there. Why don't you go over and say hello?"

Gaby turned to her mother, a bit horrified that she'd made such a suggestion. "All right, but please don't just stand here watching us," she finally replied.

"I'll be outside," Shirley said then turned on her heel and left the way she'd come in.

Gaby gracefully approached the piano with the ease of a runway model. Franklin abided his heart beating in his chest and stared intently at the keys, keenly aware of each of her approaching steps. She arrived and sat down beside him as if they were old acquaintances, her manner relaxed and confident.

"Do you play?" she asked.

"No," he said glancing nervously to meet her eyes which were looking at him. "I'm just messing around."

He realized she was more beautiful up close than she had been from across the room.

"I know chopsticks," Franklin daringly quipped. He began playing with his two index fingers.

Gaby smiled. "I think I know the other part…keep playing." A moment later she dropped in perfectly on the upper register using her right hand.

Franklin started laughing as they played it out. Then Gaby laughed with him as they played another round. Franklin sneaked peaks at her, and she caught him doing so as she peaked back, all the while holding course on the song.

They both ended in sync at the natural conclusion of the second round.

"That was good!" Franklin said, taken by her stunning blue eyes that rested easily upon him. He was overwhelmed at her presence, nervous but captivated, the enchantment of the moment playing out as if from a story.

"It was fun," she said. "My name is Gaby. Who are you?"

"I'm Franklin," he said, a bit more anxious about having to do his part in this conversation which he hoped would never end.

"Are you on the team, Franklin?"

"Yeah, first year."

"So you're going to be a tenth-grader?"

"Yeah."

"Lucky, you. I'm just going into the ninth grade at Le Conte...one more year till high school."

Franklin waxed with surprise. "Le Conte? I just graduated from there."

Gaby focused on him, puzzled. "I've been going there since the seventh grade. I don't ever remember seeing you around school."

"Uh, well, I transferred in just before I graduated."

"Oh, you just moved here?"

"Yeah...kind of like that. You want to get something to drink?"

"Sure," she said, smiling.

They walked together out to the yard and each took a cup of lemonade from the table. Franklin was oblivious to everything but her closeness to him.

"There's a bench," Gaby said, looking to the corner of the yard where the ornamental seat for two stood in the midst of a flower garden. "Would you like to go sit down?"

"Okay," Franklin half-stammered.

They made their way through the people and headed for the bench. Jeff stood talking to some friends as he caught sight of his sister walking with Franklin. He watched them walk to the edge of the yard and sit down. Shirley had viewed every move her daughter had made since emerging from the parlor. Francis, who was talking to some of the other fathers, took notice, moving slightly to his right to have an unobstructed view of his daughter sitting with the boy he'd never seen before.

They sat quietly for a moment, sipping their lemonade. Franklin realized he'd better come up with something to say, lest she think him a dolt.

"Who are you here with?" he abruptly asked.

"My parents and my brother. I think you already saw my mom. She came into the room with me when you were at the piano. She's right over there."

Gaby pointed to Shirley across the yard who smiled as she realized she was being pointed out. "That's my father over there," Gaby continued, "And my brother Jeff is over there with his girlfriend, Wendy. She's a cheerleader."

Franklin stared for a moment. "Jeff DesEnfants is your brother?"

"Yes."

"He's our quarterback!"

"Yes, I know."

"He's a good player," Franklin said, as if giving her the inside scoop.

Gaby laughed. "He sure acts like it. I hope it works."

Franklin grinned. "It might."

"What position do you play, Franklin?"

"I play on the line…tackle on offense, then end or tackle on the defense. I don't know which I'll get to play…or if I'll get to play very much. I think I'm doing pretty good, but I'm not sure about it yet. My brother Brian is really good. He's a team captain. That's him over there," Franklin said, pointing. "He's a senior."

Gaby stared for a moment. "He looks like he would be your brother," she said. "Are you all set for Tuesday?"

*So Too My Love*

"What's Tuesday?"

"The first day of school, silly."

Franklin donned a serious look. "Oh yeah, I know. Sure, I'm ready," he said with manufactured confidence, then changed the subject "Our first game is in two weeks. I hope I get to play in it. Coach said they had to apply for a waiver because I'm not fifteen yet and there's some city rule that says you have to be fifteen to play in a varsity game."

"When will you turn fifteen?" Gaby asked.

"On September sixteenth. It's just a couple days after the game."

Gaby looked into Franklin's green eyes as he turned his head to meet her gaze. "I turn fourteen tomorrow...September fourth," she said. "We'll be the same age for twelve days!"

"Hey, how about that! Born in the same month. Must be a good sign or something."

Her voice softened. "Yes, it might be."

Franklin looked at her, taken with the way she had just spoken. The sunlight sparkled off her long hair like a subtle celebration of fireworks that warmed him with the charm of the moment.

"Will you be going to the first game?" he asked. "It's a home game."

"Oh yes. I'll be going to all the games. I'll even see a little of your practices each day. The school bus drops me off right at the corner by your practice field. I'll be walking by on my way home."

"Really!" Franklin said excitedly. "That's boss."

Through the wrought-iron front gates he glimpsed the car roll slowly by and pull to the side. "I have to go...my mom's here," Franklin said, disappointed.

Gaby looked to where Franklin's eyes had turned. She saw the black Lincoln. Franklin stood up and turned to her. "It sure was nice to meet you and talk to you. Happy Birthday tomorrow. I hope I see you again soon."

Gaby stood up before him and offered her hand in a gentle handshake. "Thank you. I really enjoyed our visit. I'm sure we'll run into each other again. Goodbye for now."

Franklin shook her hand easily, aware of the softness of her skin and the sedation of her valediction. He smiled as he released her hand and turned toward the gate.

"Are you going to get your brother?' she asked, thinking he must have forgotten.

He turned back, happy for the chance at a moment more. "No, he rode with a friend," he replied. "Bye Gaby."

"Goodbye, Franklin."

Only a few seconds passed before Jeff's girlfriend, Wendy, swept in like the great oracle of all things romantic. "Well, well. It looks like you've made a new friend…a cute one, too. Do you like him?"

Gaby looked at Wendy a little befuddled. "He was nice. His name is Franklin."

Wendy's eyes calculated. "I know…that's his brother, Brian, right over there."

"I know, he told me."

"Are you going to see him again? Did he get your phone number?"

Wendy looked closely and picked up the hint of regret on Gaby's face as she answered, "No, his mom came and he had to leave. But, I'm sure we'll see each other again sometime."

# 11

Franklin remained wide-eyed as he journeyed through his first day of high school. The Quad, an outdoor area where the mass of students hung out before school and during breaks, offered nothing short of a happening where kids could buy inexpensive cinnamon crumb rolls and juice or milk, then stand around and gawk at each other. At lunch, the menu changed and the gawking intensified. Franklin missed the morning gawking, predisposed with trying to determine where each of his classes was located. But he eagerly partook in the noon session and noted the upper classmen standing about in groups ranging from two to ten, the larger groups heavily represented by members of the various fall sports teams and clubs.

Franklin stood with Drew Johnson, his best buddy from elementary school, the two of them now reunited after Franklin's solo adventures through junior high. Drew's folks had recently divorced and his mother had moved north to Hollywood with Drew and his two sisters.

Drew took a bite of his burrito and spoke as he chewed. "How were your morning classes?"

"Alright," Franklin replied. "Stinkin' math class worries me already."

Drew swallowed his bite. "I got some dickhead named Desmond for English. Dr. Desmond…a real asswipe."

"Geez!" Franklin exclaimed. "I've got him next period."

Drew chuckled. "You'll wanna kick his ass inside of five minutes. Acts like he's king of your life. He already laid a shitload of work on us."

"Terrific, can't wait."

Franklin saw Jeff's girlfriend, Wendy, walking toward where he and Drew were standing. Her stride had purpose and she was looking at him, which he thought peculiar since he didn't really know her. She stopped in front of them.

"Hi, I'm Wendy," she announced, extending a hand toward Franklin for a handshake. "You're Franklin aren't you?"

"That's me," Franklin replied, shaking her hand.

Drew recognized she wanted to talk to Franklin. "I'll see you later, man," he said as he began to walk away.

"Later on," Franklin replied.

"Bye," Wendy offered, glad that he was leaving so that she could get right down to business. She didn't waste any more time. "Did you have a good time at the Angelo's party?" she slyly asked.

"Yeah, it was fun."

Wendy gave him an inquisitive look. "I saw you talking to my boyfriend's sister…Gaby. She told me later she really likes you."

"She did?" Franklin asked, trying not to sound as excited as he was. He smiled. "I liked her, too."

Wendy flashed the pen like a magic trick. "You want her phone number? I know she'd like you to call her."

"Really? She told you that?"

"Thaaaaat's right," Wendy chimed. "Here, give me your arm."

Franklin extended his arm to her and watched as she wrote the number down his forearm like she was designing a billboard.

"Take it easy there," Franklin said too late. "I look like an art project now."

Wendy giggled, "She wouldn't want you to lose it. You should call her tonight."

Franklin went to his locker where he wrote Gaby's number down on a piece of paper. Then he went and washed the ink off his arm the best he could before heading to Dr. Desmond's class, the dickhead.

*So Too My Love*

Later that afternoon at football practice, Franklin listened patiently as Coach Birnbaum spoke to the second team linemen about the importance of the offensive line's timing in releasing to the play-side on a screen play.

"You can't be too early or too late," Coach Birnbaum explained. "Here's a timing trick. Just say to yourself, 'Ten thousand Swedes ran through the weeds at the Battle of Copenhagen' then release to the outside. All right, let's try it again."

The ball was snapped and the guys up front broke into poem, "Ten thousand Swedes ran through the weeds at the Battle of Copenhagen!" they recited loudly before releasing to their outside blocking assignments.

Coach Birnbaum chuckled. "Good on the timing, men, but say the words silently to yourselves."

Jeff suddenly yelled out, "Hey Franklin! Therrrr's Gaby!"

Everybody turned and looked at Gaby who had gotten off the school bus and was walking up the street next to the field carrying her books. Even Gaby had heard Jeff yell out. She kept her eyes forward to avoid the embarrassment of her brother's antics. As some of the guys laughed, Franklin considered running Jeff over, but didn't. He stood still, red-faced. Everybody in the whole stinking school knew there was something between him and Gaby, he thought.

Coach Birnbaum was not amused. "Take a lap DesEnfants," he said to Jeff.

As Jeff took off running, Franklin called after him, "Go get 'em track star."

After practice, Franklin exited the locker room and ran in to Wendy. She'd just finished cheerleader practice and was waiting for him.

"Gaby's out by the field. I thought you might like to know," she said.

"Thanks," Franklin said, feeling like a bull being herded, but happy about the intended direction. He made his way to the field and saw her standing by herself. They smiled at each other when she caught sight of him.

"Hey, How ya doin'?" he said as he arrived.

"I'm fine. Sorry about my brother yelling out like that."

"Aw, no big deal. I was happy to see you. His girlfriend, Wendy, is sure the persistent one though. She wrote your number on my arm today in school."

Gaby gave a knowing look. "My brother's almost as bad. After you left the party, they both wanted to know everything."

"Well, I've got your phone number now. Is it alright if I call you?"

Gaby smiled warmly. "Yes...I'd like that. Just don't call after eight or my parents won't like it."

"I won't do it," Franklin said with the sincerity of scout's honor. "Have you been here long?"

"I watched about the last twenty minutes of practice."

"Really? I didn't see you."

Gaby pointed up to the stands, "I was sitting right up there."

Franklin looked a bit puzzled. "You were walking toward the Boulevard after you got off the bus."

"Uh huh, I went home and changed my clothes. I live nearby...over at the corner of Hollywood and La Brea."

"Oh yeah? That's close. I live not too far from you...on Curson, a block up from Hollywood."

"I don't know where Curson is," she said.

"It's just two blocks past Gardner...west."

Gaby nodded. "Yes, I know where Gardner is. You are close."

"That's good!" Franklin said. They both smiled as they stood looking at each other for a long moment. "Would you like to walk a lap around the field?" Franklin asked. "It's the same lap your brother had to run after he yelled out at practice," Franklin said with a grin.

"Serves him right. Yes, let's retrace his footsteps."

They began walking slowly, side by side, each aware that it might be the beginning of something they were yet to know. Franklin's hand brushed hers, and then as if in response, hers brushed his. He let his hand swing a little wider and her hand came into full contact with his. He gently grasped her hand and held it, feeling its soft contours as her fingers closed around the edge of his hand in a reciprocal grasp. They looked at each other, their eyes speaking a mix of excitement and solemnity in the stillness of being alone together.

"I have to be home soon," she said as they strolled on.

"I can walk with you. It's right on my way," Franklin offered.

Gaby gave the slightest squeeze to his hand. "That would be nice."

At the end of the lap they left the field and headed toward Hollywood Boulevard, their pace casual as they walked and talked, unhurried in the way they moved and the words they spoke. Each of them recounted their first day back at school, and then Gaby spoke of her family, of her mother and father and three brothers.

"I guess I better watch myself," Franklin said with a smile upon hearing that she and Jeff had two older brothers.

Gaby laughed, "I guess you better."

They turned west on Hollywood Boulevard and walked past the Roosevelt Hotel. Franklin grew a bit anxious at the expected telling of his own family. What would she think about his divorced parents? And what if she wanted to hear all about him growing up? Would he tell her that he'd been expelled from several schools? What would she think of him then? The conversation drifted another direction when Gaby commented about the many moves her family had made while she was growing up.

"You lived in New York?" Franklin asked enthusiastically when she first mentioned it. He knew the Empire State Building was there, and New York was where they filmed West Side Story. "Wow! That must have been something. Did your dad get a job there or something?"

"Yes, for a little while," she answered. "I like it much better here. It was so crowded and stacked up there. Everything went straight up…tall buildings everywhere. You had to hold your head back to see the sky."

"I'd sure like to go one time…stand on top of the Empire State Building," Franklin said.

"Have you lived here all of your life?" Gaby asked, wanting to give him a chance to talk about himself and hear about him.

"In Los Angeles, yeah," Franklin answered, "But we've only been living here in Hollywood for a couple of years."

Franklin decided to give her the generic version, at least until they were better acquainted. He told her his parents were divorced, but left out the reasons why. Then he spoke about his mother and said that she was a lawyer, and he spoke of his sisters and his brother and his cousins and grandparents, and finally about their dog, Wolfgang, a long-haired dachshund that Franklin had literally grown up with.

"He's the same age as me," Franklin said, amazed at it. "He's starting to have trouble getting up the front steps of our house. We've been carrying him up lately."

"I wouldn't wonder. He's about a hundred years old in dog years. I'd like to meet him sometime," Gaby said as she stopped walking.

Franklin looked confused for a moment, having lost all thought of where they were.

"This is where I live," Gaby announced as she looked up to the second floor of the two-story apartment building. "That's our balcony right up there."

Franklin stared upward and read the name on the face of the building. "The Pacifica," he said, surprised. "I've walked by here a ton of times. I worked part-time at Hollywood Liquor right there on the corner this summer. We were almost right next door to each other. I can't believe I never saw you before."

Gaby's eyes grew wide with Franklin's telling of it. "I've been in there lots of times to buy a pop. Isn't that weird we never ran into each other?" she said.

"Well, we have now," Franklin replied, smiling. "I'll call you tonight."

"I'll be waiting. Goodbye," she said then walked through the lobby doors and into her building.

Franklin turned and ran west down Hollywood Boulevard towards home, wanting to feel the wind in his face along with the warmth in his heart. Later that night, they talked on the phone for an hour, rambling on about whatever goofy thing popped into their minds, just happy of the conversation and the chance to be connected. He walked her home the next day after practice and then again the day after.

"Would you like to come up?" Gaby asked when they arrived at her building. "My mom, and brother, Billy, and grandmother, Tedda, are here right now. I think they all want to meet you."

"Okay," Franklin replied, dubious.

"Don't worry…they won't bite," Gaby offered reassuringly.

Nobody did bite, Franklin soon discovered. Quite to the contrary, Gaby's mother had the nicest disposition, as did grandmother Tedda. And brother Billy was easy going, with no evil eye or battery of questions.

"Are you hungry, Franklin? I can make you a sandwich," Shirley said as though she would find great pleasure in doing so.

"Oh, no, ma'am. I'll be having dinner soon."

Shirley was unconvinced. "A boy your size must be hungry after all that work in football practice. I'll bet you can eat a sandwich and all your dinner, too."

Franklin knew the truth of her statement but politely declined her offer. Shirley and grandmother Tedda both took turns at the interrogation. They were so easy and demure in their posturing of each question that Franklin barely realized he was getting the third degree. Gaby helped deflect some of it, cutting in when she sensed anything she thought might be too pressing.

After twenty minutes or so, Franklin announced that he better get going. He bid his polite farewell.

"Come back again soon," Shirley said. "I know Gaby's father is anxious to meet you."

"Yes...thank you, I will," Franklin said a bit nervously at the mention of Gaby's father.

"I'll walk you out," Gaby said.

Once outside, they walked around the corner of the building away from the traffic on the boulevard and any curious eyes which Gaby thought might be watching from above. They stood looking at each other for a long moment, mindful they'd never yet kissed and aware that the time might be at hand.

Franklin had kissed a few girls before but felt gutless at the moment. He wasn't sure what she'd think, and he liked her so much. "I'd really like to kiss you right now but I have a cold," he lamely said.

Gaby didn't miss a heartbeat. "It's alright, I have a cold, too."

Frozen momentarily with the surprise of her declaration, Franklin finally stepped to her and took her in his arms then kissed her softly, their lips moving together in a lingering twinkling of first exploration and desire. They came apart for a moment, looking at each other before returning to another kiss that became more passionate. Each felt the soul-stirring moment, swept away together on the winds of life and chance to a new feeling neither had ever experienced before, an unleashing of overwhelming allure to each other. When their lips parted they stood stunned, the irresistible crush of it melding their spirits together, their heated bodies seemingly given to something higher. They each knew it.

# 12

When they were not in school or committed to something else beyond their control, they were together. From her bus drop, Gaby walked home after school each day then came back to watch the last bit of football practice, after which Franklin walked her home again. Then each evening they spoke on the phone, endlessly when they could, though sometimes driven from it when somebody else wanted to use the phone.

Their first Saturday together, Franklin came to her home and met her father, Francis. He had a wry sense of humor and peppered Franklin with talk of football and Hollywood's prospects for a good season. Franklin liked him and grew comfortable with all her family, soon feeling and acting just like part of the clan. They were kind and accepting, filling him with a sense of family which had become rare for him. After they all had lunch together, Franklin and Gaby took their leave and strolled east along Hollywood Boulevard for several miles, talking and window shopping, and occasionally walking into a store to see this or that. The next day, they did it all over again, walking the boulevard and sneaking an occasional kiss. Franklin had never been quite so happy in all his life.

* * * *

Gaby's whole family came to watch Jeff play in Hollywood's season opener, a home game against University High School. Gaby held most interest in watching Franklin, who started at defensive tackle and played some offensive tackle, too. Jeff and Franklin both played well, as did Brian who tore it up like the senior, captain ass-

*So Too My Love*

kicker he was. The team played good football, and Hollywood won 19-0. After the game Franklin met Gaby's oldest brother, Frankie, and his wife Sandy. Franklin's mother, Nancy, was also in attendance and met Gaby and her family for the first time. Franklin and Gaby were relieved to see the meeting go so well, as everyone was happy and getting along wonderfully. Nothing like good weather and a victory to raise everyone's spirits, Franklin thought. Any curiosity and inquisitiveness about each other's families seemed to have been satiated in a most delightful way.

The football season continued to go well. Hollywood won most of their games, and came close in the few they lost. One of their defeats came on the road against a non-league opponent, Manual Arts High School, which resided in the predominantly black neighborhood of south-central Los Angeles. Local riots plagued the area just weeks before the game, and Manual Arts fans were excited at the prospect of playing the expected soft, white-bread boys from tinsel town. Manual's defensive line had gained much notoriety because they were bigger than the Los Angeles Rams' defensive line, averaging 315 pounds per man, a fact which became a feature story in the sports section of the Los Angeles Times.

On the day of the game, tension in the area was still high from the recent riots. Coach Birnbaum had his team put their helmets on as the bus rolled the last mile to the Manual Arts stadium. A shot from a pellet gun hit the bus windshield, splintering the glass where it hit just as they pulled up abreast of a stadium entrance. Coach Birnbaum immediately ordered his already-suited-up team to hustle off the bus and run into the stadium. Like an evacuation drill, the team hurried off the bus, each player breaking into a run upon exiting the last bus step, then continuing immediately into an open corridor which served as an entrance/exit in the middle of the home stands. Straight on in through a gated fence and across the track the team ran, amid taunts from some already in the stands or by the gate as the team entered.

"Whitey gonna get some today...uh huh!" came the shout from a Manual Arts fan. His comment was accompanied by a barrage of similar chants, taunts, and goading insults from other Manual Arts fans, mostly loaded with race baiting and attempted intimidation. Replies from a few of the Hollywood boys quickly rang out as they made their way to the field.

"Shove it up your ass," Brian conversationally declared as he jogged by one bystander who called him a "honky cracker."

Frank Carlisi offered a more succinct reply. "Fuck you, nigger," he said with no more malice than a casual rebuff to the attempted intimidation. Of Italian heritage, Frank was a pure street fighter with the heart of a champion and unwavering toughness. If Frank got in a fight, the only thing that would keep him from winning is if he were unconscious; he kept coming, always, until he'd pummeled his unfortunate opponent. He'd had his nose broken a few times and took his share of stitches, and on one occasion was stabbed twice, but he never quit and he never lost. His knuckles were permanently swollen and disfigured from the number of times they'd been broken. With blonde hair and hazel eyes, his stature of five foot eleven, 170 pounds belied his deadly serious intent when he was challenged. He wasn't particularly talented as a football player, but started at defensive end because he was such a relentless brawler whose tackles frequently resembled attempts to disembowel or decapitate the ball carrier. He and Brian were best friends.

Franklin held awe just to be a part of it. Once the game started, Franklin noted that Manual's huge defensive line generally resembled a chorus line of Pillsbury dough boys. Their heaviest player weighed 400 pounds and moved with glacial speed, his pants belted and taped up for good measure to avoid the unsightly plague of plumber's crack every time he got in his stance. Early on, Franklin got to play some

*So Too My Love*

offense and noted the oingo-boingo effect of slamming into such mass, the physics of it cementing the notion of inertia and immovable objects. But Franklin knew the big men couldn't make tackles if he stuck to them like Ahab on the great whale.

Some of the Manual Arts players ran their mouths but ceased doing so early on in the game when it became clear that they would get as good as they gave. The scoring went back and forth. Hollywood hung tough and had the lead a few times. With conga drums in the stands to lay down the rhythm for their entertaining cheers, the Manual fans worried of the outcome. Manual would eventually win the game, but their final conversion to embattled respect of the Hollywood team came near the end of the third quarter when Hollywood faced a third down and eight from their own twenty-five yard line.

The situation looked dire for Hollywood as Manual momentarily held the momentum. Franklin stood watching from the sideline and heard the Manual fans' anticipation of the coming play build like the onset of an earthquake, the bleachers shaking as the many voices rolled together in thunderous support of their defense. Jeff took the snap from center and dropped back to pass. The Manual defensive line rumbled slowly after him, seemingly unaware that not being blocked at the line of scrimmage held a purpose. Franklin watched with reverence as his brother drifted to a spot just behind the center and waited for the ball on the tackle-eligible, middle screen play. Jeff flipped the ball over the outstretched arms of the oncoming rushers; the pass a soft, high arching wobbler that came down perfectly into Brian's waiting hands. Brian turned up field, straight-armed a linebacker in the forehead, and began running as the Hollywood offensive linemen scrambled to make blocks which turned out to be unnecessary. Brian passed his blockers and ran over two more Manual linebackers. Then he took aim at the cornerbacks and safeties who had broken from their coverage of Hollywood's receivers in surprised realization that Hollywood's star lineman had caught the ball behind the line of scrimmage and was ominously coming their way.

The contingent of Hollywood fans, which included Gaby and her parents, leapt to their feet. "Go…go… go!" they hollered.

"Run 'em over, Brian!" Frank Carlisi yelled from the sideline.

The rest of the Hollywood sideline began jumping and yelling as Brian broke into the open field and headed toward the Manual defensive backs. Brian was already fatigued from the game, being a two way starter who never came off the field. He didn't have the juice left to try juking anybody with a move. Instead, he just charged ahead with relentless defiance. Franklin watched it unfold like a dream, surreal as it continued, the possibility of his brother completing the seventy-five yard gauntlet becoming more likely as the seconds held captive in the compelling magnificence of it. One by one, Brian ran over the remaining Manual defenders as a statement of his will. He shook the last Manual defender from his exhausted body at the ten yard line then crossed the goal line in a drained jog. The Hollywood fans went berserk. The Manual fans sat stunned before some began to clap, knowing they'd witnessed a truly exceptional play.

When the game ended, Hollywood players departed the field to sincere shouts of "Good game!" from some of the same Manual fans who'd taunted them before the game.

# 13

The changing of seasons is subtle in Los Angeles. Autumn is not marked by leaves of gold, red, yellow and orange which drop to the ground or are blown from branches on blustery days to barriers where they pile deeply as a prelude to coming snows. Only the cooling air with its moisture that chills to the bone marks the waning of autumn in the City of the Angels. For Franklin and Gaby, the autumn of 1967 had been the ripest of seasons as their love blossomed, fulfilling first love for each in a passion of senses new and ever-present.

Football season ended in November, providing time for Franklin and Gaby to be together directly after school. And it came to be that they ended up at Franklin's house with privacy, inviting the final act of discovery in the bounds of their declared love for one another. Their first experience held an earnestness of spirit and commitment which overcame the awkwardness of the act. But, within weeks, all awkwardness and pretense was gone. They took to each other whenever the opportunity presented itself, often running up Curson and laughing in anticipation, then arriving at his room where they continued to laugh as they quickly threw their clothes off and fell together in heated bliss. It was fresh, this lovemaking, this physical act that became a need, a voracious itch not fraught with any moral imperative which could overcome their childlike absence of sagacity.

The joy of their relationship did nothing to foster any new outlook on school by Franklin. He hated it. His skill level and knowledge were zippity-do-dah, virtually non-existent. And he had not an iota of desire to enact any remedy. When he attended classes he felt wholly inadequate, so he frequently skipped, forging his mother's signature on excuse notes. At the end of the first semester, his grades rendered him ineligible for sports the second semester. He had wanted to join the track team and try the shot put. Instead, he got an afterschool job as a fry cook at Kentucky Fried Chicken on Vine Street, just south of Sunset. Having money in his pocket was nice and brought the opportunity for more adventure when he and Gaby went out. Though his job he enjoyed, he took notice of being ineligible for track and knew he'd have to step up his school effort to be eligible for the next football season. Gaby, on the other hand, was an excellent student. She studied hard, did her homework, and attended school every day. She was a straight A student. None of it rubbed off on Franklin.

At the end of the school year, he failed several classes. Franklin received word that he would have to pass two summer school classes in order to be eligible for football. Summer came alive with the challenge of his job, school, training, and the respite of being with Gaby. Once again, his deep desire to play football spurred a work-ethos; he attended every class and handed in every assignment. After giving what he thought was his best effort in summer school, he eked out two C's. He was proud to become eligible and embarked upon his junior year excited for football and in love with Gaby. She would be at Hollywood High with him now, even if they didn't have any classes together. They could have taken Geometry together if Franklin had dared get near it. But, he didn't, opting instead for the most basic math class available.

The year held other excitement, too. Nancy, who had been practicing law as an attorney for nine years, was appointed to the municipal bench by Governor Ronald Reagan. She looked the part in her black robe and quickly earned the respect of the local legal community, proving herself as a no-nonsense judge with exceptional judicial intellect.

The Hollywood High Sheiks opened the 1968 campaign at home against Woodrow Wilson High School, a non-league opponent from northeast of downtown L.A. Jeff was a senior quarterback, and the prospects for a good season rested in no small part on his shoulders. Expectations were high for Franklin, too. He entered his junior campaign at six-foot three inches, and 205 pounds. Coach Birnbaum hoped Franklin could pick up the slack for the absence of his brother, Brian, who had graduated. It was a challenge Franklin relished. Hollywood had a decent team. Hopes held high.

Early in the game against Wilson High, the collective wind went out of Hollywood's sails when Jeff suffered a season-ending injury to his left knee while being tackled. He initially got up and hobbled back to the huddle, waving off Coach Birnbaum's call for him to come out of the game. Just a few plays later, Jeff planted his left foot to throw and his knee collapsed with no defenders even near him. Jeff was helped off the field as groans rattled from the home stands. Everyone knew it was bad. Jeff's parents were devastated, particularly Francis who fully envisioned a college football career for his son. The game, and perhaps the season, seemed momentarily lost. But hope soon returned. Jeff's sophomore back-up, Bill Flannigan, played through his jitters, eventually getting his sea legs and throwing a pair of touchdown passes that sparked Hollywood to a win.

The mood was grim around Gaby's house after the verdict on Jeff's injury became fully known. Jeff had several ruptured ligaments. Surgery was scheduled. Jeff endured the harsh disappointment in losing his senior year. After a few more games, it became apparent that Hollywood's new, young quarterback could not replicate his initial magic, though he hung tough and showed promise.

The team struggled. The worst of it came under the lights on a Friday night against Polytechnic High School, a San Fernando Valley football powerhouse. Hollywood's players were excited to travel out to the valley and play a night game, a rarity for them. But it turned out to be a night to forget. The Poly Parrots dismantled the Hollywood Sheiks, beating them badly in a game marred by several player fights and ejections. Poly would go on to play in the City Championship Game, losing the title game by a whisker to Gardena High School. Hollywood ended the season with five wins and four losses, a respectable showing but not nearly what fans had hoped for before Jeff went down.

After the season, Franklin regressed to old bad habits, taking particular delight in tall boy Colt 45's and other alcoholic beverages. On the night before the last day of the semester, one of Franklin's good friends had a notion they should get drunk before school. The next morning they partook in several screwdrivers before first period. Franklin took the remainder of the pint bottle of vodka to class with him, pulling it from his waist and gulping away whenever the teacher turned to the blackboard. Minutes later, the teacher handed back the graded final exams, informing the class that failing the final meant failing the class. Franklin stared at his paper dumbfounded that he had failed the final by a single point. It took a minute to permeate his inebriation. Then he turned incredulous. "This is ridiculous!" he bellowed from the back of the room. Miss Vera Vignes was a young, diminutive woman with a pageboy haircut who had been teaching high school English for only a few years. She looked up in shock at Franklin who had wadded his test paper into a ball and launched it to the front of the room.

"Bullshit!" Franklin added for good measure, laughing at the perceived absurdity of it all.

Miss Vignes immediately ran across the hall to fetch Mr. Speigelman, a senior English teacher who came running when she called out, "Help!"

Mr. Speigelman arrived with Miss Vignes declaring, "He's out of control!" She was pointing at Franklin who was already standing to take his leave.

*So Too My Love*

"Come out of the class, Franklin," Mr. Speigelman ordered.

"Sure, Hawkeye!" Franklin replied with amusement. He didn't care and he wasn't mad.

Mr. Speigelman was known as Hawkeye to some because of the one glass eye that he reportedly had. Chris Burg, a wise-guy student would often yell across the Quad from a sea of students whenever he spied Speigelman entering the Administration Building. "Hey Hawkeye!" Chris would yell with the intonation and growl of a pirate. Speigelman's head would snap around and survey the crowd too late to identify the culprit.

Franklin breezed into the hall where Mr. Speigelman was waiting for him.

"It figures it would be you," Speigelman said. "Let's go to Mr. Beck's office...right now!"

Franklin began walking down the hall in the direction Speigelman wanted him to go, but Speigelman made the mistake of walking up alongside Franklin and grabbing his arm with a pinching grip. Franklin was no longer amused. He turned and bull rushed Speigelman into a bank of lockers. Speigelman slammed hard and wheezed with a look of shock.

"Keep your fucking hands off me," Franklin said with contempt.

Speigelman didn't move. Franklin began walking the other way, toward the exit closest to the street. Teachers and students alike were craning their heads out of classrooms from up and down the hall.

"What the fuck are you looking at?" Franklin challenged to those who were looking. "Fuck you. Fuck all of you."

Heads quickly pulled back in as he strode to the exit and made his way out into crisp air of early winter, the sky blue and buoyant with what life might bring. He had made it through a year and a half at Hollywood, and he knew he would not be returning. He was defeated once again.

# 14

The next day, Franklin went to an Army recruiting office and tried to enlist. The Vietnam War remained in full bloom, and the enlistment officer looked delighted to see the physically impressive lad before him. But, the meeting was short-lived once Franklin disclosed he was not quite sixteen and a half years of age.

"Come right on back when you turn seventeen," the recruiter said. "We'll be waitin' for you."

"Okay," Franklin said, deflated.

Franklin didn't mention his probable expulsion from school to his mother. After all, he hadn't been back, and no communication of any sort had been forthcoming from the school. Hollywood High didn't bother with any contact until ten days later when a letter arrived addressed to his mother. The letter was official and informed her that Franklin had been expelled. Nancy was angry and terribly disappointed in her son, but she was most incensed that nobody from Hollywood had called her or attempted any contact in the intervening ten days between the incident and the letter she stood holding.

Franklin wished he could attend Polytechnic High School, the football powerhouse which resided out of district for Franklin. Hollywood administration helped pave the way to Poly after Nancy threatened legal action over their delayed notification. Polytechnic sat fifteen miles from where Franklin lived, straight north out the Hollywood Freeway to Roscoe Boulevard on the east side of the San Fernando Valley. It was an enormous high school with nearly four thousand kids who covered all demographics in grades ten through twelve. Franklin procured his first car, a 1960 Ford Fairlane wagon. It was a five hundred dollar easy payment

*So Too My Love*

special; a beater which ran well enough to make the daily run out to the valley and back.

He held gratitude for the chance to play his senior year of football at Poly. Their team was talented, well respected, and a top contender to win the Los Angeles Championship. Poly's head football coach, Al Richards, welcomed the noted lineman from Hollywood into his program. Coach Richards was the right man at the right time. Middle-aged and fit with the look of a drill sergeant, Al Richards was tough, fair, demanding, non-judgmental, and even-keeled. All he wanted was one's best effort, and he didn't bother with ridicule or brow beating to bring such forth. His methods held a higher calling, an ability to communicate with hard cases in a manner which inspired intrinsic reform. Like a tonic, he was good for Franklin, who once again resolved to quit screwing up. Franklin understood his luck to have landed with another great coach, having departed from the magnificent Louis Birnbaum. Now he arrived to the superlative Al Richards, another coach of exceptional temperament and ability. Coach Richards also served as the head coach of the Poly track team. By some miracle, Franklin was immediately eligible to compete in track for Poly. He went out for the shot put.

As pleased as Franklin was for the chance to attend Polytechnic, Gaby abided heartbreak. She wouldn't be seeing him at school or after school. His time would be spent practicing with the Poly track team and competing at far-off track meets which she had no way of attending. She sensed their relationship would slide. And, it did. They saw much less of each other during the spring semester as Franklin's time became taken with school and practice and track meets and new friends. He worked on weekends, delivering liquor for the Liquor Locker on Sunset Boulevard. They talked on the phone and got together when they could, but it seemed to her that his friends came first more and more. She knew happiness for his success in track though she felt not a part of it; Franklin set a new school record in the shot put and finished second in Los Angeles in the event. All of it was terribly hard for her and wonderfully new for him. He loved her, but his immaturity now manifested itself as selfishness and thoughtlessness; nothing new for him, but certainly different for them.

Things improved between Gaby and Franklin when summer arrived, the summer of 1969. They spent more time together, going to the beach and movies and just hanging out. Gaby and her family had moved from the apartment in Hollywood to a house on Kling Street in North Hollywood. Franklin spent a lot of his free time at the Kling house. Gaby and Jeff were the last two siblings living at home, along with grandmother Tedda, and Francis and Shirley. Brothers Billy and Frankie, and a host of family friends, came to the Kling house for poker parties that happened weekly. Nobody loved a poker game more than Shirley. Her coy, demure style of playing became known to all, and it worked. She took more than her share of hands, laughing infectiously in a soft, high-pitched tone that exuded her love of it all.

For Franklin, the summer excited as a prelude to his upcoming senior year, not that he gave school a second thought. School was a means to an end, an end which allowed him to play football and put the shot for the track team. He had worked just hard enough to be eligible for football without having to go to summer school. When summer arrived he added more time to his work schedule, delivering liquor in Hollywood and the Hollywood hills. It was fun work with good tips and occasional deliveries to stars' homes.

One evening, Franklin delivered a large order to a gay drag party. As he carried in the order, he spotted a popular English teacher from Hollywood High dressed in queenie garb. Franklin kept his eyes forward and walked straight ahead, noticing from the corner of his eye that the teacher had recognized him. The teacher made an immediate beeline to a corner of the room where he stood hiding behind other attendees. Franklin made another trip to carry in the rest of the order, making sure his eyes were averted so as not to bust him out. Everybody at Hollywood High had known for years.

\* \* \* \*

It was the second week of August when she told him. They laid on their backs on a blanket, wistfully looking up from under the giant magnolia tree, their picnic basket close by and mostly empty now. The day was hot and the shade exquisite.

"I'm late," she said, her delivery a bit clipped from the procrastination she'd endured to the moment.

Franklin lay still, stuffed with chicken and biscuits, his attention consumed with a blue jay hopping from branch to branch. Her statement finally registered.

"What do you mean?"

Gaby turned her head and looked at him, surprised that he apparently hadn't understood. It had been a topic more than once in their two years together. And she knew what it meant this time. She'd been nauseous for a week now.

Comprehension hit him. He turned his eyes to hers then rolled to his side facing her, his head propped on his elbow.

"You're late? No kidding? How late?"

"About a week now."

"Oh," Franklin said with a measure of relief. "It'll be along soon…a week's nothin'. You've been that late before," he added confidently.

She didn't hesitate. "I think I'm pregnant. I've been sick to my stomach a few times in the morning. I've never had that before."

Franklin became fully attentive to the impact of what she'd just said. She would be the one to know, and she seemed certain. He took her hand in his.

"Oh boy," he said. "I guess we better find out for sure. How do we go about that?"

"Wendy said I can go to her sister's doctor. He's cool with it. She already asked him."

Franklin's rolled his eyes. "You told her?"

"I had to. There's nowhere else I can go without telling my folks. She won't breathe a word. She promised me"

"Yeah, okay," Franklin said. "Well, set it up and we'll go."

# 15

At his football physical Franklin weighed in at 232 pounds and measured six feet, four inches tall. He'd come a long ways since his sophomore year at six-two, 170 pounds. Reporting in top condition was a challenge achieved, but he presently couldn't find the joy in the larger picture of anything. Practice started in a week and a crisis was looming.

She stood peering out the window; nervously looking up the street, hoping his car would come into view before another minute passed. Gaby did not want to be late or even a tiny bit rushed. Not today. Only seconds more passed before she saw him coming.

"I'm going now…bye," Gaby called out toward the kitchen as she trotted to the front door.

"Goodbye, dear. Have fun…enjoy the show," Shirley replied.

"Uh huh," Gaby said, struck by her mother's unknown incongruity of sentiments. She closed the door behind her and walked quickly across the lawn to his car.

The drive to the doctor's office waxed strangely somber. Their shared mood of concern and uncertainty hung in the August heat, sweltering with thoughts run wild in an atmosphere of adultness foreign to each.

"I love you," he said as he shut the engine off in the parking spot.

She looked at him with moist eyes that held fear. "I love you, too," she said, softly.

They walked into the building and found the office. Both of them sensed the calculating stares they drew from the others in the waiting room as they stepped to the receptionist.

"My name is Gabrielle DesEnfants. I have a ten-thirty appointment with Doctor Newell."

The young receptionist looked up at both of them. "Yes Mrs. DesEnfants, he'll be right with you. If you will just fill out this paperwork and sign at the bottom, please."

She handed Gaby the clipboard. A few minutes later when Franklin returned the questionnaire to the desk, mostly completed, he said, "I'll be paying cash for the appointment today."

"Yes, I see the notation…that will be fine," the receptionist replied. Franklin reached in his pocket and dug out his money.

Twenty minutes later they called Gaby in. Franklin spent the next half an hour thumbing mindlessly through magazines which held no interest and did little to keep his thoughts from being engulfed with the coming verdict. Gaby finally walked back through the door, her face non-committal as Franklin instantly tried to read her. He rose to his feet and they immediately left the office without words. Franklin didn't bother asking. He knew she'd be informing him in just moments more as they walked for the building exit. Outside in the bright sunshine she abruptly stopped.

"I'm pregnant," she said, stunned at her own words. "He said I'm about a month along and would have the baby around May first."

Franklin stood dumbfounded, feeling an involuntary quiver pass through his body. "Nothin' like the springtime," he said, emptily.

They drove to Sizzler's Restaurant and picked at their lunches as though looking for a solution in amongst the fixings. Two nights earlier, they had talked about what to do if the doctor confirmed a pregnancy. Their conversation had eventually landed on abortion. But such talk had been easier two nights ago when the topic was a hypothetical question of 'what if?' Now it was a fact of 'what was'. Franklin broached it.

"I talked to Art Aragon last night. I got the information on the place…phone, address, and how to set it up. It's in downtown L.A.

It costs four hundred bucks. He said he'd loan it to me and I could pay him back in payments."

Art Aragon was a colorful personality who'd had a good professional boxing career before opening up a bail bonds business. Aragon Bail Bonds had been established for a number of years. Art knew all the ins and outs of Los Angeles. He had become a friend of Nancy's, visiting their house several times and telling Franklin to call him if he ever needed anything. Art seemed surprised when Franklin did call, but, good to his word, he soon had the connection for what Franklin sought. And, Art agreed not to tell Nancy.

"I'm not saying that's what we do," Franklin added. "But it's there if that's what we decide."

Gaby was forlorn and resigned to the heart breaking possibility. "I don't know what to do," she said. "I'd have to quit school if I had a baby. But it's our baby. I should tell my mom and see what she says. I'm not telling my dad...not right now...maybe never – but I want to talk to my mom. She won't say anything to him if that's what we do."

"Sure," Franklin said.

Gaby confided in her mother. Once Shirley got over the jolt of the news, she tiptoed to pragmatic consideration of her daughter's future. Shirley was old school, of an era when unmarried girls in trouble were shamed and stigmatized. Even in the cultural revolution of the late sixties, she understood her daughter would receive harsh judgment. The decision of abortion arrived like a high-speed train hitting a sharp bend in the tracks, the physics of circumstance too rapid to avoid a catastrophic derailment. The abortion was planned.

Gray is the sky which hangs on such a decided event, like the rotting of the soul as conscience languishes in the squalidness of a dark corner turned, putrid in decay, unpurified by sunlight of cause, as the cause was venal and theirs alone, mocking their love in an eclipse of purpose and faith, and levying a coarse indifference damned to regret.

The building resided in an older, mostly dilapidated, industrial section of downtown proper. The faded exterior of block and steel showed visible rust where colorless enamel had long since peeled from window frames, giving it the vacant appearance of a time passed on. Shirley accompanied Franklin and Gaby. She wanted to be present for her daughter. Franklin was grateful for the additional support. After all, he didn't have to go through what Gaby was about to, not physically at least. He had no idea of what to expect in the aftermath for her, physically and emotionally. Shirley's presence could help with what might come.

They entered and walked down a long, dim hallway that led past empty office space. At the end of the hall Franklin found the suite number he sought. The title on the glass door simply said, 'Medical', confirming what Franklin had known from the moment he had spotted the address and parked the car; the place was a dump, befitting the grim occasion. The interior of the office did nothing to inspire new confidence as Franklin, Gaby, and Shirley were met by a middle-aged woman dressed in tired looking medical garb. A fine coat of dust covered everything in the place. The office appeared unkempt, and smelled peculiarly dank with a wisp of formaldehyde.

"Are you Franklin?" the woman asked.

"Yes," he replied.

"I'll let the provider know you're here," she said then promptly disappeared through a door.

Franklin looked at Gaby who stood stoically silent, though was unable to conceal her underlying expression of muted terror. Shirley didn't look much better. Franklin stood paralyzed for a moment until the decision hit him like a revelation.

"We're not doing this...let's go," he said matter of factly, taking Gaby's arm to lead her out the door.

"What are we going to do?" Gaby asked, confused.

"I'm not sure but we'll figure it out," Franklin replied. "Let's get out of here."

That was good enough for Shirley and Gaby who both walked briskly out the door as Franklin held it open. It felt like an escape from a nightmare.

Franklin drove up the on-ramp and headed for the Hollywood Freeway, bound for Gaby's house. Gaby sat next to him, close. Shirley sat in the back seat. None of them had said anything since departing the appointment which turned out to be the only thing aborted that day. Several miles down the freeway, Franklin spoke up.

"We'll get married and raise our child. I'll get a full-time job," he declared.

Gaby looked at him, surprised and momentarily speechless. Shirley beat her to a response, immediately chiming from behind them, "That would be wonderful!"

"Can we even get married?" Gaby asked. "Are we old enough?"

Franklin frowned in consideration. "I don't know for sure."

"The laws are different in different states," Shirley said. "I'm sure there's somewhere that you could."

"Yeah," Franklin agreed. "We'll find out which state it's legal in and go there."

Gaby smiled, her face relenting from the fear, confusion and anxiety which the day had so far produced. "Do you really want to? Or are you just saying that?" she asked.

"I really want to. We'll do it right away."

She squeezed his leg. "I love you," she said, only loud enough for him to hear.

"What was that?" Shirley asked, not wanting to be left out of anything at this point.

Franklin cocked his head toward the back seat. "She said you might like to go to Hamburger Hamlet for lunch. Then we could walk right over to C.C. Browns for a hot fudge sundae for dessert."

Shirley gave a high-pitched laugh. "She didn't tell you all that. I saw her lips move…she only said two or three words."

"You don't like the idea…Hamburger Hamlet and C.C. Browns?" Franklin asked as if the offer might be rescinded.

"Well, I should say I do," Shirley replied, laughing again.

# 16

Shirley did not tell Francis that their daughter had almost gotten an abortion. It was a good thing. He broke angry when told that Gaby was pregnant, but immediately declared that abortion was out of the question. "It's a sin against God," he said. His fury became mildly pacified upon learning of his daughter and Franklin's plan to marry immediately.

Franklin and Gaby went to the library in search of reference books which could tell them of age requirements in each state. She was just days away from turning sixteen, and him only weeks shy of seventeen. Their investigation soon made it clear that they could marry in Nevada, and a few other states, if each had parental consent. Otherwise, he would have to be eighteen. Such would not be an issue for Gaby, but it meant that Franklin would have to tell his mother of Gaby's pregnancy if he hoped to secure her consent. He felt reasonably sure his mother would agree, so they grew excited at the prospect of a trip to Las Vegas and one of the countless wedding chapels that resided there. Francis and Shirley liked the plan, too, drawn to the thrill of the desert oasis with its promise of good times to be had. Franklin would talk to his mother right away.

Nancy didn't have to give their plan much thought to arrive at an answer. "You can't even take care of yourself and you want to be responsible for a wife and child at your age?" she said, thick with rhetorical tone. "It would be an unmitigated disaster. I will not consent to it."

Franklin kept at it, putting forth his most mature and reasoned self. "Mom I can do it," he pleaded. "I'll quit school and work full-time…and we can live with her parents until we can afford our own place. They already said it would be all right. I love her."

"I'm sorry, hon. I can't agree. You two would never last. In the meantime you both would be throwing your futures away. Marriage is hard enough for adults. You're just kids. There are much better alternatives. She could give the baby up for adoption."

"Mother, please."

"No."

The news didn't go down well on Franklin's next visit to Gaby's house, especially with Francis. "Get out of my house!" he ordered Franklin. "You are not to see my daughter anymore."

Gaby cried and yelled at her father while Shirley sat silently, distraught at the unfolding events. Franklin left. He called Gaby's house later that night. Gaby answered the phone.

"Hi love," Franklin said. "Has it calmed down any?"

"Not much. My dad's really mad. He says I'm grounded and I'm not supposed to talk to you right now. He's acting crazy. It's all such a mess."

"I'll try my mom again, but I don't know," Franklin said.

"You better not call here for a while. I'll call you. I love you."

"I love you, too."

Football practice held relief. Just a few days earlier he was going to quit school, get married and not look back. Now he sweated in the heat, pouring himself into it and the exhaustive, tranquil beauty of it, happy to be on a good team. The end of Hell Week had arrived when the man showed up at Franklin's door one afternoon. The man wore a tie and appeared to be middle aged.

"Are you Franklin?" he asked.

"Yeah."

The man, flipped open the wallet he held, revealing an L.A.P.D. badge and police identification card. "I'm detective Tom

Lapley of the Los Angeles Police Department. Are either of your parents at home?"

Franklin stood speechless for a moment, trying to think of anything criminal he might have done lately. "Uh...no. They're divorced. I live with my mom. She's not here right now."

"All right," he said. "I'll contact her later to inform her of my visit and its purpose. How old are you, Franklin?"

"Sixteen."

The detective's eyes widened a bit. "Do you know Mr. Francis DesEnfants?"

"Yeah, he's my girlfriend's father."

"I'm here to tell you that Mr. DesEnfants has sworn out a criminal complaint against you for statutory rape of his daughter. He's says she's pregnant and you're the father. Is that right?"

Franklin stood taken aback. "Yeah...but I never raped her."

"That doesn't matter. She's a minor and considered by law not to have the capacity to consent to sex. If I arrest you, you'll be charged with a felony. It could be reduced to a misdemeanor, but I don't think you want to risk that, do you?"

Franklin shook his head. "I don't know what that means. Are you going to arrest me?"

"That's up to you. I spoke to her father. He doesn't want you around his daughter anymore. If you stay away from her, I won't arrest you and he won't press the issue. If you don't heed this warning, you'll be arrested and charged with statutory rape. Is that clear? Do yourself a favor, son. Stay away from her. Here's my card. If you have any other questions, call me at that number."

The detective turned and started down the front stairs to his car. Franklin felt like he'd been gut-kicked, a flush of emotions running through him. He was mad, he was hurt, he felt betrayed by her father and confused at what had just happened. Mostly he was just grim with the surge of old feelings from his accumulated failures and screw-ups. The next football practice couldn't come soon enough.

Gaby called him that night. She was crying. "I can't believe he did that," she kept saying.

"Well, he did," Franklin said, his tone resigned to the fact. "I can't see you. Not now. Maybe some time after a while. I don't know. I love you. Call me when he's not around."

"I will…when I can. I love you."

\* \* \* \*

Time is serene, forgiving in its passage like a storm that yields, a color that fades, a tree that dies, as all things under heaven are given up to that which follows, everlastingly nascent. So it is in the movement of all things that evolution runs of God's hand.

The frequency of Franklin and Gaby's phone conversations waned with the seeming futility of trying to be together. Slowly their lives grew increasingly independent of each other, particularly Franklin's. Letting go was infinitely easier for him. He had other pursuits which demanded much of his time and effort, primarily football season, to be followed by track season. Gaby had only to wonder how much longer she could attend school before her prolonged leave of absence and the relative loss of her adolescence to motherhood. Her imagination would include all of the experiences and opportunities a girl of her age would be missing.

Franklin proved incapable of appreciating her plight and the depth of her anguish as she faced losing her chances, and the boy she loved. But, she was tough, a child who had worked professionally to support her family. Without complaint, she was up to the task, growing more and more determined to make the best for her coming child and herself. She and Franklin saw each other secretly a few times, only to realize their drift from what they had once been together.

# 17

Franklin was consumed with football as the Polytechnic Parrots rolled over their opponents one by one in crushing fashion, headed toward a regular season finale with their league rival, the San Fernando High School Tigers. It would be cruel irony that the two best teams in Los Angeles resided in the same league that year. Only the league champion would advance to the playoffs. Both teams entered the last game undefeated, setting the stage for a showdown which had been anticipated the entire season. San Fernando's quarterback, Anthony Davis, aka A.D., seemed really to be just a sensational running back that played quarterback, taking shotgun snaps and running wild on sweep plays. Poly had a star running back of its own, Bill Kramer. The night turned into a rushing extravaganza, seesawing back and forth in a pure thriller with A.D. gaining 221 yards and Kramer gaining 228. Trailing by one point, San Fernando scored in the last minute of the game to win 20-14. They went on to win the L.A. City Championship, and Franklin could only yield to contemplation of what might have been. Anthony Davis went on to star at USC.

Track season turned out better for Franklin. He continued to break his own school record and set a new league record of 58-9. Then he placed first in the City Finals to become the Los Angeles City Champion in the shot put. During the same fortnight, on May 7, 1970, Gaby gave birth to an eight pound, eleven and a half ounce boy one minute before noon. She named him Matthew William DesEnfants, picking the name Matthew after Franklin's brother, Brian, had casually suggested it to her once.

Franklin went to the hospital for the joyous event. A throng of high school girls also attended, jubilant and excited as if at a gala premier. Franklin visited with Gaby for only a minute or so, feeling awkward in the presence of her father and the rest of the family, all of whom who were at the hospital. Through the glass of the nursery window he stared at his infant son for half an hour, mesmerized by the helpless creation which he and Gaby had conceived and she had birthed. A calm clarity of the miracle overtook him, soothing him like nothing else ever had. It would be a year gone by before Franklin would look upon his son again. His circumstances accelerated in another direction.

From nowhere they came, football people inquiring of him. He had worked hard and played well but was awestruck at all the sudden attention. Many of the letters and phone calls came from places Franklin had only heard of. Oklahoma, Nebraska, Michigan, LSU, and a host of others got in touch, including most of the PAC-8 schools and hometown UCLA and USC. The downpour of attention quickly evaporated when the disaster of his high school transcripts became known. Nobody could get him in with a 0.8 GPA. Only one path existed to continue playing football. Franklin would go to Junior College.

Then Arizona State contacted him and insisted they could get him in immediately. Franklin flew to Tempe on a weekend recruiting trip and spent two hours with an assistant coach who showed him the campus and the stadium while expounding on the success and upward trajectory of their program. Afterward, the coach introduced Franklin to his host, Mike Tomco, a current all-conference tackle on the team. Mike would be Franklin's guide and entertainment director for the rest of the weekend.

"You'll like the car you're in tonight," the coach said to Franklin as he and Mike were leaving the coach's office.

"That's a fact!" Mike declared.

*So Too My Love*

Once outside, Mike started filling Franklin in. "They must want you pretty bad. I got two hundred for our spending money. It's usually a hundred. And set your eyes on that bad boy," Mike said, nodding to the Oldsmobile 442 convertible that was parked just ahead. "This baby hauls ass! Coach said it was a pace car for some race."

"Outta sight," Franklin said as he climbed in.

Mike gave Franklin a tour of the town and delivered the usual perfunctory praise about the program. But Mike talked with genuine respect about Head Coach Frank Kush, whom he praised as an outstanding coach. The sincere words about Coach Kush impressed Franklin. Coach Kush had departed town for the weekend, so Franklin would not get to meet him.

After a short tour of the sights, Mike sprang the idea. "Hey, you wanna go to Mexico? Down to Nogales? We could be there in two hours. It's a kick."

"Mexico?" Franklin said with a tone of adventure. "You're the host...Arriba! Arriba! Andele!"

"All right! You're going to fit in great here. You'll love it."

Mike swung by the market and picked up a big cooler and bags of ice, then hit the Liquor store for a case of beer. With the top down and the radio loud they headed south through the desert, the heat shimmering and the sun hanging as an orange globe low on the horizon. Mexico lived wild and the night held long. They arrived back in Tempe after daybreak.

At the end of the weekend Franklin met with the recruiting coach once again in his office. After a few formalities, the coach smiled at Franklin and made his pitch.

"How'd you like that car?" he asked.

"That thing was fine!" Franklin boasted.

"Well, that will be your car if you come to school here. How 'bout it, Franklin? Coach Kush and all of us would like you to become a Sun Devil."

"If you can get me in right now, I'd love to come here," Franklin replied.

A broad smile came to the coach's face. "Good deal! That's outstanding! Coach Kush will be very pleased." The coach extended his hand. Franklin shook it with the vigor of a young man who'd just won a sweepstakes.

The humor faded some from the coach's expression. "Now, you'll have to take an SAT test since you haven't done so yet," he said. "All you have to do is get a minimum score on it and we can get you admitted on a hardship status. We'll set up the test-date time in Los Angeles, and we'll arrange a tutor for you. You'll have to take the test by the end of June to be eligible for fall admission, so you'll need to take full advantage of the next few weeks to prepare yourself. Are you ready?" the coach asked with a final burst of enthusiasm.

"Sure," Franklin answered, feeling duped. He knew he could not pass such a test with a few weeks preparation, tutor be damned. Nevertheless he was willing to at least entertain the possibility and give it a go. So he prepped with the tutor several times a week, which seemed only to confirm the worst. In the end, it wasn't even close. He sure would miss that Olds 442.

With junior college as his only option, Franklin made his plans. Brian had attended L.A. Valley College and played two years as a Monarch for the popular JUCO near Van Nuys. Now Brian had received a full ride to UCLA and would be playing football for the Bruins in the fall. Franklin chose Los Angeles City College over Valley, primarily because they gave him a job running their weight room, and their head coach, Ron Botchan, recruited him and his Poly teammate, Bill Kramer, very aggressively. So Franklin and Bill both went to LACC. The demographics were vastly different from Valley College; LACC's football team was predominantly black. Franklin and Bill were two of only three white starters offensively,

*So Too My Love*

but they became the best of friends with their teammates and ended the very successful season as the team's two most honored players.

That same season, 1970, Brian played his junior year as a starting guard for the UCLA Bruins who had a winning season under Head Coach Tommy Prothro. Coach Prothro left his six-year tenure at the end of the 1970 season to become the head coach of the Los Angeles Rams. Brian would play his senior year for a new coach.

UCLA wanted to secure Franklin to their program, so they came to him shortly after his season with LACC to enlist him to their plan. UCLA proposed that Franklin transfer to Santa Monica City College and sit out his second year of football in order to have three years of major college eligibility remaining when he transferred to UCLA.

UCLA's offensive line coach, Tony Kopay, explained it to Franklin. "You just show up for your classes and we'll take care of the rest. Dale Ride is the Dean of Students and he'll make sure you take the right courses with the right instructors. He's a good guy and a big supporter of our program...a lot of the professors there are. You'll like it at Santa Monica."

Franklin had become a big UCLA fan because his brother played for them. He had every intention of playing there, too. UCLA facilitated the transfer to Santa Monica, and Franklin sat out the next football season. He attended his classes and took the opportunity to see all of UCLA's home games, watching Brian play his senior year under new Head Coach, Pepper Rodgers, from Kansas. Brian played terrifically, but UCLA struggled badly under their new head coach.

"You don't want to go there," Brian told his younger brother at the end of UCLA's sufferable season. "Rodgers is pretty goofy. I don't think he'll do very well."

Other schools were still aggressively recruiting Franklin. Now he started to pay attention to them, particularly Cal and Colorado. He took several recruiting trips each to Berkeley and Boulder but kept it all on the lowdown since he was beholding to UCLA's help and gratuities at Santa Monica. Franklin wasn't sure what he'd do or where he'd go, but he certainly enjoyed those recruiting trips.

# 18

In 1971, Franklin attended Santa Monica City College while Gaby lived at home in North Hollywood and continued raising Matthew as a full-time mother. She and Franklin saw each other twice that year. The first occasion came in early February when they snuck away together once. In the darkness just before dawn they were asleep in each other's arms when the bed began weirdly jumping around the room. The Sylmar earthquake rocked much of Los Angeles like the final jolt of their slim prospects together. Then in the pastel blue of an easy spring day, May 7, Franklin showed up to Matthew's first birthday party held at North Hollywood Park. For Gaby and Franklin the happy occasion abided a melancholy ache as they said simple hello's to each other, giving face to a platonic reality, and finding only solo joy in watching their son's beaming face.

    That same year, Nancy gave marriage one more go-round when she wed Philip E. Watson. He held the office of Los Angeles County Assessor. After they were married, Nancy moved in with Philip and put the Curson house on the market. Nine-year old youngest sister, Diane, moved with Nancy and Philip, too. Diane's new step-father adopted her and she took the last name of Watson. Franklin didn't care much for Philip but was grateful for his mother's new found happiness, so he steered clear of him. Soon after they married, Nancy ran for an open seat on the Los Angeles Superior Court and was elected. As a superior court judge, Nancy became part of several high profile cases during her career, arraigning Tex Watson, Patricia Krenwinkle, and Leslie Van Houten of the murdering Manson family, and serving as the trial judge for Muharem Kurbegovic, infamously known as the Alphabet Bomber.

When the Curson house sold, Franklin moved into a small house in Hollywood with Frank Carlisi, Norman Price and Priscilla Price. Franklin had just recently met Norman and Priscilla who were brother and sister, both of them serene in the era of hippies. They were completely ingratiating, wonderful people. With Frank Carlisi and Franklin being more akin to Cro-Magnon young warriors, it was an interesting assemblage of housemates that turned out to be an excellent mosaic as they all became great friends.

Franklin and Frank made their money at night working as rock concert security for an outfit called Peace Power. They worked all the big shows and venues in Los Angeles, including the Hollywood Bowl, Greek Theatre, Santa Monica Civic Auditorium, The Palladium, The Forum, and a host of others. A private security firm, Peace Power employed between twenty and fifty personnel at each show. They kept the peace with a strong presence and swift, physical action if needed. Peace Power quickly developed a bad rap and condemnation on local FM radio stations, nevertheless continued to be employed because they proved effective and managed to avoid any catastrophic incidents. Working in front of the stage could be a challenge as overzealous attendees occasionally tried to rush and mount the stage, resulting in take-downs, punch outs, or the offenders simply being flung off the front of the stage to land as they might. The occasional sucker-punch was thrown by some attendees and could result in serious beatings for those who did it. But the worst of the fights and beatings happened in the hills behind the back walls of the Hollywood Bowl and Greek Theatre where Peace Power personnel were charged with keeping people from sneaking in. From the darkness of the hills, would-be gate crashers threw bottles and cans at Peace Power workers. Franklin and Frank had been hit in the body by thrown objects, leaving bad bruises. Franklin narrowly missed being hit in the head a number of times.

*So Too My Love*

One hot night, Franklin stood stationed at a rear corner of the Greek Theatre just beyond the back wall in the hills. Unexpectedly he heard the yells piercing the darkness. "Franklin! Franklin!" The panicked shouts came from the opposite corner of the back wall where Frank Carlisi was stationed. Franklin sprang to a run through the bushes and trees in the direction of where his friend was in obvious distress some 100 feet away. The calls kept ringing out as Franklin closed the distance. He finally came to a clearing where he could see Frank ahead, being held against a tree by two large males. A third thug was swinging away, hitting Frank in the face, head and body over and over again. Frank kicked and cursed as he took the beating.

Franklin arrived at a dead run and swung his heavy magflashlight with brutal intent. The flashlight exploded on the head of the puncher who instantly collapsed in a heap. Then it became two on two as Frank and Franklin threw hard and fast, quickly getting the upper hand in a beating. Frank's opponent soon escaped and ran bleeding up the hill, so Frank turned his attention to Franklin's opponent. Franklin had his rat bastard in a headlock with his left arm while he rained punches to his head with his right fist. Franklin was surprised when he heard the rat bastard's high-pitched scream as Frank bit a hunk of flesh from his side. Working for Peace Power sometimes turned out to be more adventurous than they bargained for, but the money was good and the work came steady.

\* \* \* \*

As the year 1971 faded, the silence between Franklin and Gaby marked their separate paths. They had migrated emotionally beyond reach of each other. Franklin became romantically involved with his housemate, Priscilla. Gaby began dating Rick Seavert; a former friend of Franklin's who had gone to Vietnam for a year as a Marine after being offered the choice between the service and jail. He was a handsome kid with charm who had returned from the war deeply affected and in search of normalcy. Neither Gaby nor Franklin knew of each other's activities. They no longer mixed with common friends.

Priscilla was a few years older than Franklin. Her two older sisters, Patty and Pam were married to band mates Richie Hayward and Lowell George of the band Little Feat. Richie was married to Pam, and Lowell to Patty. The three sisters were close, so Franklin ended up becoming good friends with Lowell and Richie, attending family gatherings and parties together. Franklin also spent many evenings watching the band rehearse in a giant sound stage at Warner Brothers Studios in Burbank. He liked the music and they liked talking football.

In the spring of 1972, as Franklin closed in on the end of his junior college requirement, USC began recruiting him diligently, offering him posh living arrangements and other financial enticements. He went to dinner with USC Coach Craig Fertig several times and happily partook in the best steak and prime rib he'd ever had, all in USC neighborhoods which offered a refreshing if sobering contrast to UCLA's Westwood. But Franklin had deeply disliked USC for the two years that his brother had played at UCLA. He decided it was out of the question to play for USC.

Franklin began leaning heavily toward Colorado. The Buffaloes had finished the 71' season ranked number three in the nation, and his recruiting trips to Boulder had been inspiring times in the most beautiful of settings; the Rocky Mountains and the spectacular Flatirons that rimmed the university as an incomparable backdrop. Devil's Thumb, a pronounced formation of conglomerate sandstone which resembles a hand's base digit in a hitch-hiking bid for a ride over the Rockies, sits in the southwestern horizon from the east stands of Folsom Field, like an exclamation point atop the broad, magnificent expanse of The Flatirons' enormous walls. Boulder's

*So Too My Love*

beauty held in stark contrast to the stale congestion of Los Angeles. The atmosphere of the high country kindled the romance of nature in Franklin. For their part, CU remained relentless in their pursuit and determination to put the best offer on the table. CU's biggest booster, Bob Six, the President and CEO of Continental Airlines, teamed with Coach Jim Mora to wine and dine Franklin on a frequent basis. Mr. Six had Franklin up to his Bel Air home for dinner with him and his wife, Audrey Meadows. Franklin was overwhelmed in their company, but they put him at ease with their graciousness and simple manner. He thought them the best of folks.

Mr. Six crafted financial enticements for Franklin, which included a job offer and an arranged price for all of Franklin's complimentary football tickets. And CU would provide free housing off campus in addition to his full scholarship and monthly stipend. It became easy to say 'yes' and brought relief to be done with the process.

Franklin had been to Boulder once again the final weekend before the National Letter of Intent deadline. He returned to Los Angeles International Airport on Sunday evening, accompanied by Coach Mora who would sign him the next day at Nancy and Philip's house, an occasion which would also be attended by Mr. Six.

Franklin was uncommonly happy as he and Coach Mora left the plane and walked down the corridor to the end of the gate where people waited for friends or relatives. Franklin's good mood suddenly turned to mortification as he spotted the familiar face in the crowd ahead, a face whose expression looked as if it were witnessing a murder. Standing there with his eyes locked on Franklin was UCLA's offensive line coach, Tony Kopay.

"What are you doing?" Coach Kopay blurted out to Franklin with a tone that implied treason.

Franklin couldn't believe it. *What in the hell is he doing here? How could he know I was arriving on this flight?* Franklin thought.

No matter now. He was here. Franklin and Coach Kopay looked at each other like The Society of Disbelievers.

Franklin turned to Coach Mora who appeared to be having his own Maalox moment. "Uh…excuse me a minute, Coach," Franklin said to Coach Mora.

"Take your time," Coach Mora replied then quickly walked away, happy to escape the discomfort of the moment.

Franklin turned back and stepped to Coach Kopay. "I'm sorry, Coach…I'm signing with Colorado," he said.

Coach Kopay looked incredulous. "How could you do that? What about all the things we've done for you – arranged for you?"

Franklin felt the heat on the back of his neck. "Well, yeah, I really appreciate all of it, Coach, but I'm going to Colorado."

# 19

In 1972, Boulder, Colorado remained thick with the counterculture residue of the late sixties, the hippie-gypsy movement having metastasized from both coasts to places inland, fertile with the right cultural soil while being aesthetically alluring. Boulder fit the bill perfectly. Young people couldn't walk the two blocks of The Hill without being approached by several of the homeless-hippie looking drug dealers selling weed, whites, reds, Quaaludes, acid, and other products currently in demand in the People's Shire of Boulder. A historic district immediately west of the university, The Hill was home to Tulagi's, The Sink, and other assorted eclectic establishments as well as a mass of CU students, many of whom lived in fraternity and sorority houses in neighborhoods directly adjacent to The Hill. Most anybody of age who ever spent appreciable time in Boulder frequented The Hill at least once in a while, perhaps to attend one of the house or block parties which were common. CU football players generally preferred to hang at more downhome places like The Broken Drum, Walt and Hanks, Tom's, or the Hi-Lo out on the Diagonal. Franklin would soon find the football team to be the alternate universe to the liberal freak show that was Boulder.

    He arrived in Boulder in July and moved into a house on 19th Street, which CU provided. Priscilla accompanied him on the drive up from L.A. She stayed for a visit, one of several before their long distance relationship eventually yielded to the geographic divide.

    Not long after Franklin moved to Colorado, Gaby married Rick Seavert on August 3, 1972, in Las Vegas, Nevada. The ceremony occurred at one of the infinitum wedding chapels Vegas is famous for, the same kind in which Franklin and Gaby had planned to be married three years earlier. It was a low key affair. Francis and Shirley were present as was brother, Bill, who stood as Best Man to Rick. Rick's sister, Becky, stood as Gaby's Maid of Honor. Gaby and Rick spent an additional night in Vegas before returning to L.A. where they and her two-year-old son, Matthew, promptly moved into a small apartment in Van Nuys.

\* \* \* \*

For Franklin, adjusting to the overwhelming magnitude of Division 1 college football became a thrilling reality. CU played to sold-out venues at home and on the road in the storied Big-8 Conference, made up of Nebraska, Oklahoma, Oklahoma State, Missouri, Kansas, Kansas State, Iowa State and the CU Buffaloes. During Franklin's time at CU, he played in other great venues, too. CU traveled to non-conference games at places like Ann Arbor, Baton Rouge, Madison, Minneapolis, and the ever-inspiring Air Force Academy.

In December, 1972, CU played Auburn in the Gator Bowl, a fiasco of a game which marked the beginning of the end for CU head coach Eddie Crowder's coaching career. The week preceding the game became tainted with embarrassing team incidents. Several Gator Bowl Association cars were driven into the surf of Daytona Beach by CU players who apparently couldn't get the hang of driving on the beach. Next, a CU player jumped to a palm tree which looked close enough to his fifth story balcony. He made the jump but ended up taking twenty or so stiches on the inside of his thigh, slicing it open as he slid down the palm tree fifty feet to the ground. CU moved from Daytona Beach to Jacksonville, the site of the Gator Bowl, for the last two days before the game. The team's mascot buffalo, 'Ralphie', was being housed in a temporary corral in the hotel parking lot. It happened there that CU's head trainer, a

*So Too My Love*

cherished and respected man, ended up needing therapy of his own after he climbed into the corral and tried his hand at buffalo riding during an evening's exuberance. Ralphie didn't take to the notion of being ridden. Then, at a banquet for both teams where all the players were presented Gator Bowl rings, watches, and other gifts, the captains for each team were given the opportunity to thank The Gator Bowl Association for the honorable experience and all that had been provided. The Auburn captains went first and aptly demonstrated their gracious southern manners. Next, the CU captains made their remarks, the first of whom presented his appreciation in a sincere, if not smooth, delivery. But the packed banquet hall fell silent when the next captain stepped to the microphone donned in pink leather jacket and said, "I'd just like to say that I have no comment at this time."

Not to be outdone by such profound eloquence, CU's final captain stepped up and bellowed, "Enough said already. Let's blow this pop stand!"

The following day, local press accounts baked CU with a story summed up by a label of 'no class'.

December 30, 1972 brought a cool and breezy evening under the lights at the Gator Bowl. The CU team was preceded onto the field by Ralphie who broke into a stampede run with his handlers sprinting for all they had, hanging on to his harness straps in an effort not to be dragged. Ralphie knew the drill well. His nearly ton of hair and hide thundered up the center of the field before turning at the end and returning up the Auburn sideline with folks scrambling to get the hell out of the way. The CU fans leapt to their feet, yelling and clapping for their love of the spectacle. Ralphie beheld a picture of domination, heightening the frenzied anticipation and aspirations of what was to come. But Ralphie could spur no redemption as the hapless CU Buffaloes crushed only the hopes of their fans, losing to Auburn 24-3.

The next season, 1973, Franklin embarked on his junior year and Eddie Crowder on his last as CU coach. After the embarrassing finale to the '72 season, Eddie adopted his new, unwritten, 'honesty policy'. If Eddie didn't think you were honest, you wouldn't be playing. Several star players coming into their senior seasons were no longer starters, and a few of them didn't even make the traveling squad. These were some of the same players who had contributed greatly to CU's road wins against LSU and Ohio State, resulting in CU's number three national ranking at the end of the 1971 season.

Franklin witnessed Eddie's evolving style while at Madison, Wisconsin, where CU had traveled to play the Badgers. As chance would have it, Franklin's brother, Brian, was living in Madison and playing football for the Madison Mustangs, a semi-pro football team. Franklin and Brian had not seen each other for nearly two years. Brian called Franklin as soon as the CU team arrived at their hotel on Friday preceding the Saturday game. Franklin could not leave the hotel, so he asked his offensive line coach if he could skip the customary after-dinner movie in the banquet room and instead visit with his brother in his hotel room.

"I'd like to say yes," his coach said, "but you'll have to check with Coach Crowder on that one. You can catch him in his room right now."

Coach Crowder opened his door a few seconds after Franklin knocked on it. "Hello, Franklin. What can I do for you?"

Franklin explained that he had come to ask permission to visit with his brother. Coach Crowder invited him in then closed the door. "Now what's this all about?" Coach Crowder asked.

"Well, I haven't seen my brother in a couple of years and he's living here in Madison. I was wondering if I could skip the movie tonight and visit with him in my room instead."

Coach Crowder frowned and grimaced. "Is that an honest thing to ask? That's the problem. We can't be a team when people want to do willy-nilly whatever they like. You're asking for special treatment. You want to deviate from the plan."

Franklin was stupefied. "Well...it's just that I haven't seen my brother in a long time. What does it matter whether I watch the movie? It's just a movie."

"This has nothing to do with the movie," Coach Crowder said, his tone heavy with contempt. "It has everything to do with you not wanting to be part of the team. You think you're special. You'd let your teammates down. Your selfishness and dishonesty is a disgrace to your team."

Franklin was no longer bewildered. He was mad. "I came here to ask your permission," he said. "Now I'm telling you...I'll be in my room visiting with my brother." Franklin turned and left the room not waiting for any response.

His visit with Brian was the best. They spent several hours in Franklin's hotel room catching up and enjoying being together. The next day, Franklin retained his starting spot at right guard and the Buffaloes beat the Badgers. A few weeks later, Brian got a call from the Houston Oilers and ended up their starting guard for the rest of the season, and the following season, too.

# 20

Time tumbles down in the frenetic pace of living, the hours and days and weeks and months calving away in the glacial movement of years. Franklin and Gaby rolled with the tide of life, the highs and lows like the inanimate phenomenon of weather, producing seasons akin to the personal struggles of being, the storms and sunny skies and all manner in-between consuming the flash of living.

Gaby worked at Robinson's for a time, a retail department store. She moved on to earn better money working in the records department of a medical clinic. Soon thereafter she was promoted to the position of receptionist. Her son, Matthew, attended day-care, taking to it well and demonstrating intelligence, curiosity, and a proclivity for being a sweet and wonderful child. He was the apple of his mother's eye. Her husband, Rick, spent almost a year more as a Marine after their marriage. Then as a civilian, he landed a helper/apprentice job on a civil survey crew. But, he held trouble in his heart and preferred most anything over sobriety, so soon lost his apprenticeship. With the chaos of her husband's indulgences, Gaby held her job and her son in ultimate regard. She pressed on with a purpose only motherhood can bring.

In 1974, tragedy struck the DesEnfants family when Gaby's father, Francis, died of a sudden and massive heart attack at age forty-seven. Gaby received her mother's phone call at work and raced to the hospital. She arrived too late. His death shocked the family and quickly evolved into the most trying of times for Shirley who possessed no money of her own. She had to give up their rented place and move in with eldest son Frank Jr., his wife, Sandy, and eldest grandson, Jean Paul. After six months or so, Shirley moved in with Gaby, excited to be nearer to her daughter and her beautiful grandson, Matthew. But Shirley soon witnessed the challenges of her daughter's marriage and cared not to add to Gaby's burden, so she moved on to live with her second eldest son, Billy, who made a good living and was single. Her new living arrangement proved perfect for the time, providing an opportunity to amass some savings from the VA benefits and Social Security disability she received. Shirley had an eye toward getting her own place in the future. She did.

Late in 1974, not long after Shirley had moved out of Rick and Gaby's place, Gaby decided she'd had enough of Rick's lifestyle and roving eye. She initiated a separation and Rick moved out. About the same time, Franklin finished playing his senior year at CU. It had been a subpar season under new head coach Bill Mallory, but Franklin had been deeply honored to be voted the team's Most Valuable Player and selected to play in several college all-star games: The East-West Shrine Game, The Coaches All-America Game and The Senior Bowl.

In March, 1975, Franklin married Joan Dwulet, a girl he'd begun dating eight months earlier after having a class together at CU. She hailed from Point Pleasant, New Jersey, where the two took their vows before a crowd that included Nancy, and brother Brian who stood as best man.

Weeks later, the St. Louis Football Cardinals drafted Franklin in the fifth round of the NFL draft. He felt a bit disappointed. While at the East-West Shrine Game, Franklin had been solicited by Howard Slusher, a big-time sports agent who wanted to add Franklin to his stable of clients. Howard told Franklin that he would be a first or second round pick, laying out sample contracts with Franklin's name already imprinted, each contract showing different terms for what Franklin could expect to get if Ole Howard pitched for him.

Twenty-two years naïve, Franklin's eyes swooned with the numbers he saw before him. Yes, Howard would be his man.

After the surprise of Franklin's slip to the fifth round, Howard told Franklin he'd since learned that his former head coach Eddie Crowder had not spoken well of Franklin to all who inquired. Crowder had remained at CU as the athletic director. Other sports agents who subsequently sought Franklin as a client suggested his stock would drop if he signed on with Slusher, whom many claimed, NFL owners despised. But warnings had come too late and reasons mattered not. Franklin's slip in the draft meant he held little leverage.

Howard scoffed at St. Louis' initial offer; advising Franklin to hold out of training camp if need be, guaranteeing that St. Louis would come around to Howard's demands. Cardinal's owner Bill Bidwell was notoriously frugal. The Cardinals had the lowest payroll of any NFL team. Howard told Franklin that he, the client, had final word, though warned it would be perilous to Franklin's career if he didn't follow Howard's counsel. Franklin worried of such a position but stayed on board, putting it all in Howard's hands.

The 1975 NFL season arrived with the start of training camp, notably marked with the rookie reporting date. Franklin did not report, officially making him a holdout as a fifth round pick. A week later, Howard called to say that St Louis had increased their offer some, relaying the new numbers to Franklin. Franklin immediately pushed Howard for acceptance. Howard knew it unlikely that he'd get any more out of Mr. Bidwell. He advised Franklin to report.

The next day, Franklin flew to St. Louis and was met at the airport by former Cardinal, and soon to be Hall of Famer, Larry Wilson, who now worked in the Cardinal front office. Larry drove Franklin out to training camp, the three hour trip from Missouri to Illinois most inspiring for Franklin who sat entranced to be in the company of the legendary player. Larry was great, telling Franklin old war stories of football and the inside of things, treating him just like one of the fellas. Franklin was floating on cloud nine when they finally arrived at training camp. But his cloud was vaporized when he met Head Coach Don Coryell, who gave Franklin nothing more than a steely glare, ignoring Franklin's outstretched hand before turning and walking away without a word or hand shake.

In 1975 the NFL reduced the size of active rosters from 47 to 43 players. For Franklin, the change meant he would have to beat out two veteran offensive linemen instead of just one, to make the team. The Cardinals had won the NFC East the year before and the 'Cardiac Kids' had a supreme offensive line with solid veteran backups. Franklin was not up to the task and was released in the final cut after six pre-season games. Coach Coryell shook Franklin's hand when he broke the news to him.

"You're a very talented kid but just a little too green right now," Coryell told him. "I'm sure you'll get another shot with someone else in the near future."

Coryell turned out to be right. About a month into the regular season, Howard Slusher called. The Kansas City Chiefs had lost a guard to injury and wanted Franklin in Kansas City ASAP for a workout, and, if they liked what they saw, they would sign him immediately. After taking a physical and being put through all the paces with KC's offensive line coach at Arrowhead Stadium, Franklin was escorted to Head Coach Paul Wiggin's office where he had a cordial meeting with Coach Wiggin. The coach informed Franklin of their desire to sign him to a guaranteed, no-cut contract for the rest of the '75 season. Franklin became inwardly ecstatic. He waited in an outer office while KC worked out the deal by phone with Franklin's agent, Howard. It wasn't long before KC's General Manager came and told Franklin that Howard was on the phone and wanted to speak with Franklin. He led Franklin to a private office with a phone.

"Mr. Slusher's on line one," the GM said before closing the door as he left.

Franklin sat down and pushed the lit button. "Hello, Howard?"

"Yes, Franklin. Listen, this isn't going to work out. They're insisting on a three year deal with no signing bonus and only a twenty-five hundred dollar bump in years two and three with this year's contract being only thirty thousand. I told them we'd be happy to sign a one year deal at twenty-eight, but they won't agree to just a year. They're trying to lock you up for cheaper than cheap."

"Yeah, but they said it's a no-cut for the rest of this year," Franklin said.

"Well sure", Howard retorted. "It's robbery by carrot and stick. You have much more earning power over the next three years than what they're offering. Listen, Franklin, you're going to hear from other teams soon enough…teams that will give you a much better deal. You have to say no to this. Trust me."

As the plane began its takeoff roll, Franklin felt sick to his stomach. He had just declined an offer for immediate employment in the NFL during the regular season. His despair at what he knew to be his own stupidity slapped him repeatedly with the sting of remorse. A few weeks later, Franklin accepted a one year deal to play with the Southern California Sun of the World Football league, presently in its second year and in dire financial straits beyond what most people knew. Franklin played one home game at Anaheim Stadium, home of the Angels and now home of the Sun, too. He noted the pink jersey he wore and the fact that, as a football stadium, there wasn't a good seat in the house. The next week the league folded.

With two games left in the NFL regular season of 1975, the Denver Broncos called and made an immediate offer of twenty-five hundred dollars per game for the two remaining games, and a following year contract at considerably better money than any team had ever offered. Howard advised Franklin to take the deal, a position which Franklin had already resolved himself to.

He felt the jubilation, the new lease on life as he worked at his first practice with the team. The late fall day sparkled splendidly clear and cool to the sweat he bore and the mile high air he heaved for. But, like a dream that had to spawn imperfection, the front office messenger abruptly appeared at Franklin's side on the practice field.

"Mr. Gherke needs to see you," he stated, with no trace of humanity. "He said you should go ahead and shower and get changed before you come over."

Franklin knew nothing good could result from such a request. When he arrived at Fred Gherke's office twenty minutes later, the Broncos' General Manager invited him in, directing him to a seat.

"You played this year in the World Football League?" Gherke asked innocuously.

"Yes," Franklin answered as if he'd committed some crime. "Just one game for the Southern California Sun right before the league folded."

Gherke gave Franklin an 'oh damn' look. "Well, that's our mistake," he said. "I should have asked you earlier. The fact is you're ineligible to play in the NFL for the remainder of this season if you played in the World Football League this season. We have to void your contract for the rest of this season. But we'd like to keep next season's contract in force. We'd like you with us next year. Are you agreeable to that?"

Franklin didn't pause. "Yes, sir, there's no place I'd rather be."

"That's fine then. We're very happy to have you."

The idea instantly came to Franklin. "So you'll still need another guard now?" he asked, "Because I know where you can find a good one. My brother's available."

Mr. Gherke looked inquisitive. "Your brother?"

"Yeah, my brother, Brian. He started for the Oilers the last two years but got caught up in the coaching change this year and was waived. He played his college ball at UCLA."

Recognition registered on Gherke's face. Brian had started against the Broncos as a Houston Oiler the previous season at Mile High Stadium. "Yes, yes, I know who Brian is. He's available on short notice? You have a phone number for him?"

"Yeah, he's in L.A. He just got back from a hunting trip. He's in good shape."

And so it became. The Broncos called in Brian and signed him for the last two games of the '75 season as well as the coming '76 season. Franklin thought he and Brian might end up in training camp together the next season and be competing for a job. But, shortly after the end of the '75 season, the Broncos traded Brian to the San Francisco Forty-Niners for wide receiver, Fair Hooker. Brian informed the Forty-Niners he was retiring and would not be reporting.

Franklin moved back to Boulder with his wife, Joan, and began getting ready for the 1976 season. He worked on a trash truck and told the driver to keep rolling as he ran behind from side to side, grabbing trash cans and emptying them, completing the routes in record fashion each day. The work proved to be a fun and effective part of his training regimen. Franklin made the Broncos final roster for the 1976 season. In the best of times and grandest of adventures, Franklin played in the legendary stadiums of the league, with and against all the great players, the experience of it like a dream beyond all others.

*So Too My Love*

Shortly after the season ended, Franklin and Joan went their separate ways. Their divorce closed a short-lived marriage which was plagued by volatility and mired in superficiality. She moved back home to New Jersey.

Just about the same time, a post-season player insurrection of veteran Bronco players against the continued leadership of Head Coach John Ralston led to Ralston's dismissal. The Broncos had posted a 9-5 record for the '76 season, missing the playoffs by just a single game. But Ralston lacked the respect of the veterans who started the movement against him. One of those players was Lyle Alzado, a star defensive end who in team meetings during the season had routinely mimicked Ralston's distinct tone and nerdy inflections in a loud, sarcastic, disparaging manner. Ralston never reacted to Alzado's brazen disrespect beyond mildly saying, "Now come on Lyle...let's not have any more of that." John Ralston had been a very good coach and stood largely responsible for moving the organization forward in big steps.

Red Miller became the Broncos coach in 1977 and promptly drafted a guard in the first round; just a year after Ralston's Broncos had drafted a guard, Tom Glassic, in the first round of the '76 draft. The two first-round picks at guard in two successive years translated into Franklin being squeezed from guard to tackle, a position which was new to him, and one for which he was a bit undersized by NFL standards. He worked hard and ended up starting the last two preseason games at left tackle against Seattle and San Francisco. Then he was released in the final cut. He had played well in both games except for one play in the final pre-season game against the 49'ers when he was beaten for an assisted sack by their Pro-Bowl defensive end, Cedrick Hardman. The only thing beating Hardman to a first hit on Bronco quarterback Craig Morton was Cleveland Elam, the 49'ers defensive tackle who had simultaneously beaten left guard Tom Glassic. It seemed enough to spook Coach Miller who reconsidered the prospect of having such youth on the left side with two second year players, Glassic at guard and Franklin at tackle. Coach Miller immediately traded for a veteran tackle, Andy Mauer.

At the meeting where Franklin was officially waived, Mr. Gherke surprised Franklin with another offer. "We think you're the man of the future at tackle and expect you to have a long career with us," Gherke said. "We want to keep you on a sort of phantom squad. We'll pay you half your salary to attend all meetings and designated workouts. You could be reactivated this season if circumstances permit. What do you say? Are you agreeable to that?"

Franklin was certainly agreeable to the notion of receiving half his salary to hang around, and he liked being in Denver. "Sure...all right. Thank you," Franklin said.

Franklin's signed his new deal and endeavored to work hard with a sense of good will. But his good will flamed out the very next day when he discovered that Coach Miller had kept the player who had backed up Franklin when he was the starter. The player had been with Coach Miller before in New England and was now the back-up to the veteran tackle Miller had traded for. *Why in the hell didn't he keep me as the backup?* Franklin wondered. Why does the guy who was my backup get to remain on the active roster? Franklin became poisoned by the seeming injustice of it. His attitude deteriorated in a slow burn, and he didn't live up to his end of the bargain as he eventually began missing meetings and workouts. When the final reactivation deadline rolled around in October, the Broncos released Franklin who had worn his indifference in a manner which demonstrated disrespect. He continued to receive the remainder of his half-salary through the regular season, but he interminably suffered his fool's play when the Broncos made it to their first Super Bowl that season.

# 21

Early in 1978, the Philadelphia Eagles called Franklin to say they'd been duly impressed with his play as a Bronco against their defensive end, Carl Hairston, the year before during a preseason meeting at The Vet. They offered him a contract. Franklin signed with the Eagles and began training for his July reporting date. Hot and humid would be the east coast forecast for July; other than the weather, he didn't have much idea of what to expect. Franklin continued living in Broomfield, Colorado, taking on good friend and former CU teammate, Steve Byrne, as a roommate. Bernie had grown up in Sacramento, California but remained a transplant after his CU days had finished

Franklin worked nights as a drummer at the Bus Stop, a strip club on North Broadway in Boulder. The work paid enough money to keep his days free for the gym. The rest of his time slid to being translucently debased. As his reporting date in Philadelphia began to appear on the horizon, he planned a trip home to L.A in late May to visit his mother and other family and friends.

So came the season of spring, the time of miracles, when renewal of growth shrugs winter's dormant respite in a call of urgency to nature's notion of making hay while the sun shines. By chance he was home when his phone rang one evening.

"Hello?"

"Hello there. You know who this is?"

He knew the voice and felt immediate joy. Seven years had passed since they had spoken, yet the warmth of who it was filled his heart.

"Gaby?" he said, startled at the platonic reality. She instantly became the dearest of old friends. "It's so great to hear your voice," he said with comforted easiness. "How are you?"

"I'm well. It's nice to hear your voice, too," she said. "I'm here with Sue Seavert. She found your number and said we should call you...so I dialed. How are you? What are you doing now?"

Sue was a mutual friend and Gaby's sister-in-law, now ex sister-in-law, a fact Franklin was unaware of.

"Just working and living here in Colorado. Tell Sue hello," he said, wondering why Sue would be prompting Gaby to call him when Gaby was married to Sue's brother.

"Hi Sue," Gaby said away from the phone. Franklin could hear Sue's greeting from the background.

Gaby spoke back into the receiver. "Are you still playing football?"

"I'm trying to," he replied. "It seems I've done more trying than playing. We'll see."

Franklin told her about the Broncos and that he had recently signed with the Eagles. Then he asked her about their son, Matt. She told him all about Matthew, recounting the things he liked do and the activities of his school life. Franklin listened, enchanted by her telling of it. As the conversation continued, Franklin fell shocked and saddened to hear that her father had died in 1974. Things hadn't ended well between Franklin and Francis, but Franklin held deep affection and respect for the man who had treated him so well during the two years that he and Gaby were together. Gaby went on to say she'd been divorced from Rick for about a year.

"There's a coincidence, Franklin said. "My ex-wife and I split up a little more than a year ago, too. We didn't quite make it two years."

"Oh, I'm sorry," Gaby said.

"Don't be. It was the best thing for both of us," Franklin offered. "Hey, I'll be in L.A. in a couple of weeks. How 'bout we all get together for dinner one night...you, me, Sue, and whoever. It would be something fine to catch up face to face."

"Yes it would," Gaby agreed. "I'll give you my number. Just let me know a couple of days ahead."

They spoke for another ten minutes like old times. Then he broached the subject, the question coming of its own volition, surprising him as spoke the words. "Does Matt know who his real father is?" he asked.

Her voice sailed smoothly. "No...he knows Rick's not his real father, but he doesn't know who his father is. He just knows he's gone. I'm sure he will get more curious about it someday...but he hasn't yet," she said.

"Yeah," Franklin replied, suddenly short of thought. After a moment of silence, he got back to his impending visit to L.A. "So I'll call you when I get in and we'll get something set up."

"I'll be looking forward to it," she said.

"Me, too."

After Franklin hung up the phone, he stood for a moment, awestruck that he'd just spoken with her. He felt excited, though no thought of romance ever entered his mind or his heart. Too much time had passed. They were different people now; adults. It would just be fun to see her again and enjoy an evening together, he thought.

A few weeks later, he arrived in L.A. On an early Friday evening he drove out the familiar Ventura Freeway to the house where he would meet Gaby. Nervousness tried to settle on him as he parked the car and walked toward the front door. The approaching darkness held tranquility with warm air and fading clear sky. He glanced upward as he took a rather deep breath and rang the doorbell. Time hung for a moment before the last few footsteps hurriedly approached the door from inside. The door opened just enough to reveal the eight-year old boy, his young face beaming with blue eyes that penetrated Franklin like lasers.

"Hi buddy," Franklin said, astonished that he was toe to toe with who he instantly knew was his son. "You must be Matt," he said.

The boy with the long, blond hair showed all his teeth with a grin as he nodded. "Can I have your autograph?" he suddenly asked.

Franklin was floored by the request. '*You are my autograph*,' he thought, aware that his son knew not of his father standing before him. The irony of it was astonishing to Franklin.

"Sure you can," Franklin said with a smile. He heard more footsteps coming.

The door opened all the way to reveal her standing behind Matt. Her smile melted him. He stood taken with the starkness of her beauty, reminded of the first time he'd ever laid eyes on her from the piano eleven years earlier. She was twenty-four years old now and every bit a woman, a detail Franklin abruptly realized as if it hadn't occurred to him before this very second.

"Well hello there," she said with a style and elegance that radiated through him. "Are you going to invite our guest in, Matthew?"

"Sure I will. Come on in," Matt said as he stepped to the side.

"Thanks, Matt," Franklin said. He stepped into the house and embraced Gaby, holding her in a gentle hug. "Hello, Gabrielle. You look wonderful."

"Thank you," she said, releasing from his embrace after a moment. She regarded him with appraising eyes. "You look wonderful yourself. Wow, you've gotten so much bigger!" she said with surprise.

Franklin gave her an 'aw shucks' look. "Only thirty more pounds or so," he said. "It goes with the trade."

"I would imagine," she replied. "Well, come in and see Sue and Donny and Kelley. They're all waiting."

Spellbound, Franklin followed her and Matt through the living room toward the kitchen as if they'd just walked off with his beating heart. For the rest of the evening he continued to secretly stare in captivated amazement, trying not to be too obvious and interacting with the others there as a matter of courtesy and cover. At the end of the evening, Franklin knew he needed more. He spoke to Gaby privately out by his car.

"What are you doing tomorrow night?" he asked

She was playfully coy. "Ohh, I don't know…why?"

"Well I was thinking we could go out…get some dinner, take a drive."

"Actually, I'm off weekends and I told my mom I'd come for a visit. She's not too far from here…on Canoga Avenue. You could pick me up there."

"Okay, yeah, I'd like to see Shirley,"

"She'd really like it, too. If you want, you can come over in the afternoon. She has a nice pool at her building. We spend a lot of time poolside. Matt loves it."

"Poolside sounds fun. I'll come about two? Then we could go out later?"

"Yes," she answered, her temperament faintly reserved. "I'll call late morning at the number you gave me and give you her address and phone."

"Outstanding," Franklin replied. They stood looking at each other a moment more before stepping forward and modestly hugging, each of them slightly guarded in the face of unfolding and bewildering emotion. He got into his car and waved as he drove off. The remainder of the night swirled away, each with thoughts and events of the evening running wild in their minds before sleep.

A few minutes before two o' clock the next day, Franklin slowed his car in search of the address. He spotted Matt standing as a sentry by a driveway across the street. The boy was waiting to direct Franklin into the proper parking lot of the massive apartment complex. Franklin made the left turn across the large boulevard and pulled into the driveway, stopping by Matt who trotted to the passenger door and opened it.

"I'm here to show you where to park," Matt said as he climbed in with an' ear to ear grin.

"Great! Thank you!" Franklin said smiling back at him.

"Go down there all the way to the end," Matt said as he pointed to the right.

Franklin turned the wheel and started slowly rolling. "Aye, aye, captain."

The words jumped from Matt's mouth like they wouldn't be contained another moment. "You're my dad?" he asked as if only seeking final confirmation.

Franklin turned his eyes to his boy, hit by the sledgehammer question. "Who told you that?"

"My mom told me this morning."

Franklin put his hand to Matt's leg and gave it a gentle squeeze in the moment of truth. "That's right," he said, "I'm your dad. Is that okay with you?"

"Yeah!" Matt said. "It makes me really happy."

Franklin thought he might cry but managed not to. "Yeah, it makes me really happy, too," he replied with a crack in his voice.

# 22

The afternoon lingered sublimely as Franklin played with Matt in the pool, launching him over and over again in an astronaut game which Matt couldn't get enough of. Franklin visited with Shirley, too, her kindness and effervescent personality as present as he ever remembered. Upon an invite to dinner, Shirley refused, insisting that Franklin and Gaby go alone and enjoy their time together. Shirley coerced her grandson to remain with her for the evening and partake in pizza and ice cream. Matt happily agreed.

After dinner at a nearby restaurant, Franklin and Gaby drove out Topanga Canyon to the beach, the long, scenic drive giving them the chance to talk about everything under the stars. They did, rediscovering each other and the joy they had known in being together.

The evening was divinely transformational for Franklin. By the time they arrived back at Shirley's, things appeared crystal clear to him. He shut the car off then turned to her and kissed her. When their lips finally parted, he came right to the point.

"We belong together...we should be together," he said as if glimpsing the stone tablets which said so.

Gaby was taken aback. "What are you talking about? We just went out one time. We haven't seen each other in years."

"Exactly!" Franklin declared as if she'd just made his point. "Haven't we wasted enough time?"

Her eyes held astonishment. "You're crazy!"

"Only about you and our son," Franklin said, and then kissed her again before she could talk. The kiss was long and simmering with emotion from the words he'd just spoken, his lips melded with hers in the lingo of love. She answered his passion with her own, taken by the moment. They finally came apart.

"Come to Colorado for a visit...you and Matt. You'd love it. He would, too. I've got plenty of room. Can you get some time off?"

Gaby paused momentarily as her gaze softened. "Well, I do have some vacation time I could take...a week maybe. I could see."

"Yeah...nice!" Franklin said. "Find out. As soon as you know, I'll get the tickets. You can fly right out of Burbank."

She smiled at his excitement. "I'd have to give my boss some lead time. And Matt's not out of school for two more weeks, but maybe we could come then."

"I'm counting on it," he said, and then they kissed again.

\* \* \* \*

It was the middle of June in the Rockies, when the cool winds of spring have fully yielded to the heat of summer, the wildflowers of high mountain meadows bursting with paints that beckon design of rapture, resplendent with the animate of hummingbirds and all manner of life given to its attraction. They basked together, Franklin, Gaby and Matthew, touring the mountain standards of Estes Park and Nederland, and sharing activities far removed of an urban experience. Matthew had never been in such places. The enchantment of all that they saw and did danced magically upon him. Gaby, too, was overwhelmed by the majesty of the surroundings and the emotional gravity of them all being drawn further and further together. The week slowly gave way like the breech of a tarn, the escape of their time together settling as a delta of repose and grace. Franklin was resolved in his heart to that which he knew had to be. The night before Gaby and Matthew were to leave, he spoke to her in the stillness of the night as their son slept in the next room.

"I don't know what's going to happen with the Eagles, but when it's decided, I want us to be together...wherever that is."

Gaby held quiet for a moment, looking at him. "I love you," she said, "but I don't know if I'm *in* love with you. This has all happened so fast. You have deep feelings for me, too, but I can't imagine you're in love with me either. We're not kids anymore. We don't want to make a mistake."

His eyes bore into hers. "My whole life has been a series of mistakes. I'm damn certain this isn't one of 'em. I've never been more sure of something being right. Yeah, maybe we're not in love right now like when we were kids, but it sure feels like it. I know it's there. It's coming. You'll see."

"I'm just scared," she said. "I don't want my heart broken again. I have Matt to think about, too. He'd be crushed if things didn't work out."

Franklin's expression turned to concern. "Yeah, well, that's the only part of this that scares me," he said.

"What do you mean?" she asked.

Franklin looked uncomfortable. "I don't ever want to treat my own children the way my father was to me. It scares me that I might."

She reached out for him. "You'd be a wonderful father. I've seen the way you are with him."

"Yeah, but this is just fun time right now," Franklin said. "Showing him wonderland is easy. The hard part is living."

She smiled with understanding. "That's how it would be for all of us."

"Yes," he said. "But we have to take the chance. The biggest mistake of our lives would be if we didn't take that chance."

\* \* \* \*

The heat and humidity of Philadelphia in July was only slightly more oppressive than the reality of how many players Coach Dick Vermeil and the Eagles had brought to training camp. It was a horde, guaranteeing the most limited of repetitions for players down the totem pole. During team offense, Franklin got to run at left guard about once every sixth play. It wasn't the amount of work he needed or hoped for. He spoke with Gaby each night on a pay phone located at the end of the dormitory hall. Their conversations comforted and uplifted him, restoring him to a better spirit for the next day's challenge. But he didn't believe he could make the team with such limited work.

Two weeks into camp, Franklin went to see Coach Vermeil after practice. He came right out with it: "I'd like to be waived right now if you wouldn't mind," he said. "We haven't played any games yet and it would give me a chance to get on with somebody else...while it's still early."

Vermeil frowned. "Why don't you want to try and stick here?" he asked.

"I just don't feel like I'm getting much of a shot. There's more players here than I've ever seen. Getting reps are slim pickins for anybody other than the starters."

"Well, we've seen you," Vermeil said, half irritated. "You were the best lineman on the field in yesterday's scrimmage...and damn near the worst in today's practice. I don't quite figure you."

"I know I'm inconsistent. That's why I need more reps. I just don't see it working out here...so I was hoping you could just cut me right now."

Vermeil nodded his head slowly. "Let me think about. I'll let you know," he said.

The next day, Franklin was traded to the San Diego Chargers. He had to report immediately and boarded a late-morning flight for the west coast, surprised at the good fortune of his new destination and his first-class seat.

Gaby could hardly believe it. "You're already here?" she asked when he called her that evening.

"I sure am! It's not what I planned on when I got up this morning, but I guess sometimes things work out better than you planned. I'm in La Jolla where training camp is. The offshore breeze here is mighty fine. Yes indeed."

"You're only a few hours away now," Gaby said, excitedly. "Maybe we can see each other sometime when we're both not working."

"That won't be anytime too soon, but hey…get this…we're playing the Rams in the Coliseum in a few weeks. I'll get tickets for you and Matt. I don't know what the schedule will be yet but I'm sure we could visit for a few minutes after the game."

"Oh, that would be such fun. Matt would absolutely love it."

"Yeah, plan on it."

And so it was that a few weeks later Franklin fulfilled a long-time dream of playing in the Coliseum in his hometown, against the Rams who he had rooted for all of his life. He played three-quarters of the game at right tackle and had a very good night. It was beyond exhilarating to be under the lights with family and friends and Gaby and his son there to see it.

By the end of the preseason, Franklin had logged significant playing time in each of the six games. He believed he had played the best football of his brief NFL career and imagined he had beat out the starter. But he received word that Head Coach Tommy Prothro wanted to see him, and he soon knew the disappointment of once again being released in the final roster cut.

"You played well enough to make this team," Prothro told him, "but we have a large investment in our number two draft pick,

Milton Hardaway, so he stays instead…at least for this year. It's a tough business. Good luck to you."

Just a few days later, Franklin received an offer from the British Columbia Lions of the Canadian Football League. They offered a three year, no-cut contract. He turned it down, determined to move on with his life and not miss the boat on the one thing that mattered most to him now. He loved her and wanted a life with her and his son. It was the richest of fortune that she loved him and agreed to start a life together. They moved to Colorado and embarked on their days as a family.

Six months later they moved to their hometown Los Angeles and settled in for what may come, neither of them with any career horizons immediately beyond the menial jobs they had, but desperately happy in having each other.

Then on September 29, 1979, they were married in a small ceremony of about forty guests at Nancy and Philip's home. Judge Nancy performed the ceremony with Brian standing as Best Man, and Gaby's sister-in-law, Sandy, standing as Maid of Honor. It was not without realized sadness that Gaby's father, Francis, had not lived long enough to witness the marriage or walk his daughter to the altar, but it became the sweetest of moments when nine-year old Matthew walked in Francis' place and gave his mother away to his father.

# Epilogue

It became our glorious blessing to have two more sons in the years to come; Brian, named after his uncle, was born Thanksgiving Day, November 27, 1980. Then six years later in 1986, came Sean, also born on Thanksgiving Day, November 27, the first time since Brian's birth that Thanksgiving Day again fell on the 27th. In their years as children, moments occurred when I would watch them play or wrestle on the living room floor, captivated by the immense beauty of their being and our family's being, yet feeling fatalistic sadness in the knowledge we would all end someday, our moment in life ever fleeting and changing, as if I hoped it could all be preserved like a Rockwell painting or the happy scene inside a snow globe, the splendor of the moment captured forever. But the gift of life is precisely such because it does end, at least here on earth.

After thirty four blessed years of marriage to Gaby, and a legacy which presently includes four grandchildren, the question I asked during a moment of crisis in my youth lingers in reverberation: *What's the point of living if all you do is die in the end?* I have since come to understand that my thought revealed the fear of my mortality and the despair in my heart from the absence of God. Such questions have undoubtedly been agonizing during the history of mankind, our distant ancestors enduring unfathomable suffering from tyranny, war, affliction, illness and poverty, and on such a grand scale that today's worst circumstances in developed countries could be regarded as trivial by comparison, though there is nothing trivial about despair and suffering and the many forms of poverty that exist around the earth. His plan is incomprehensible to us, but His word is His gift and dictum for the path and conduct in our individual lives. The purpose of my life is His purpose, yet it is my marriage to Gaby and the raising of our three sons that saved me and fulfilled me with something so much larger than myself.

Because of God giving us free will, I can loathe, I can condemn, I can turn away, I sin, and I can freely come to God. His grace is perfect, His mercy infinite. Because of God, I can love, I can forgive and be forgiven, I have faith in Him, I can persevere, and I will die and dwell with Him and loved ones evermore. God was, and is, my salvation and redemption. So too was my mother, and my sisters and brother, and my children, and many others who helped sustain me with love and support. But most of all, Jesus is my anchor, and so too is Gaby; So too my love.

www.ingramcontent.com/pod-product-compliance
Lightning Source LLC
Chambersburg PA
CBHW031401040426
42444CB00005B/377